CHOPSTICKS RECIPES

VEGETARIAN DISHES

美點佳餚

養生素食

歐陽效詩編著

Published and Distributed by

Chopsticks Publications Ltd.
P.O. Box 73515, Kowloon Central Post Office, Hong Kong.
108, Boundary Street, G/F Kowloon, Hong Kong.
Tel: 3-368433   3-390454

© *Cecilia J. AU-YEUNG*

All Rights Reserved
New revised edition
2nd print May 1988

ISBN 962 7018 67 8
Photography by Wilson Au-yeung
                    Au-yeung Chiu Mei
Edited by Caroline Au-yeung

出版者及總批發
嘉饌出版有限公司
香港　九龍中央郵箱73515號
香港　九龍界限街108地下
電話：3-368433　3-390454
本書版權所有不得翻印或轉載

FOREWORD

Vegetarian dishes are becoming more and more popular, as people begin to realize the importance of eating the right food, at the right quantity. It is necessary to form good eating habits from an early age; some people found out too late that over years of eating 'trash food', they have developed high blood pressure, weak heart, obesity, etc. — such conditions are difficult to rectify at that late stage.

Vegetarian dishes do not have to be boring and insipid as most people imagine; careful planning can avoid monotony in vegetarian diets. I have published 'Chopsticks Recipes' Book 7 — Vegetarian Dishes to show that there are numerous ways of cooking nutritious vegetarian food which are both interesting and delicious. The aim is to introduce health food in Chinese cooking to lessen cholesterol, high blood pressure and heart diseases.

This book includes dishes which suit vegans, lacto vegetarians, ovo-lacto vegetarians and anyone who does not normally try vegetarian dishes. Gourmets will find that this book will add more variety to their everyday menu when they introduce our vegetarian dishes into their daily diet. Whichever of the above categories you belong to, I am sure that you will find this book most interesting and useful.

Cecilia J. Au-Yeung

CONTENTS

目錄

蠔 油 三 寶

Assorted Vegetables in
Oyster Sauce

材料：

西蘭花 6 安（168克）
椰菜花 6 安（168克）
沸水 3 杯
鹽 1 湯匙
糖 1 湯匙
菜油 3 湯匙
珍珠笋 4 安（112克）
紅蘿蔔數片
羌 2 片
葱頭 1 粒
蒜頭 1 粒

調味—鹽¼茶匙
　　　糖 1½茶匙
　　　酒 1 茶匙
　　　羌汁 1 湯匙
　　　上湯½杯
　　　蠔油 2 湯匙
　　　胡椒粉少許

饙料—生粉 1 茶匙
　　　水 1 湯匙
　　　老抽數滴
　　　蔴油 1 茶匙

製法：

*　西蘭花，椰菜花修妥洗淨切成小塊
　，放於沸水中加鹽，糖及油 1 湯匙
　飛水。撈起，過冷河後隔乾水份。
　鹽水留起候用。
*　珍珠笋及紅蘿蔔放於以上鹽水中飛
　水，過冷河隔乾留用。
*　羌片切絲。葱，蒜頭切片。
*　燒紅鑊加餘油 2 湯匙煮沸。洒下
　鹽爆香羌，葱蒜，隨即傾入椰菜花
　及西蘭花兜炒 1 分鐘，再加入珍珠
　笋及糖拌炒數下。讚酒加羌汁，倒
　入上湯及全部調味料撈勻。以生粉
　水埋饙後洒下蔴油上碟。以紅蘿蔔
　裝飾。

Ingredients:

6 oz (168 g) broccoli
6 oz (168 g) cauliflower
3 cups boiling water
1 tbsp salt
1 tbsp sugar
3 tbsp corn oil
4 oz (112 g) baby corn
a few pieces carrot
2 slices ginger
1 shallot
1 garlic clove

Seasoning-
¼ tsp salt
1½ tsp sugar
1 tsp wine
1 tbsp ginger juice
½ cup stock
2 tbsp oyster sauce
a pinch of pepper

Gravy Mix-
1 tsp cornflour
1 tbsp water
a few drops dark soy
1 tsp sesame oil

Method:

*　*Trim and cut the broccoli and cauliflower into small florets. Blanch in the boiling water with the salt, sugar and 1 tbsp of oil. Refresh and drain. Keep the boiling water for later use.*
*　*Remove the baby corn from the tin and blanch in the above salted boiling water with the carrot pieces. Refresh and drain.*
*　*Shred the ginger. Slice the shallot and garlic.*
*　*Heat the wok to bring the remaining oil to the boil. Sprinkle in the salt then sauté the ginger, shallot and garlic till aromatic. Pour in the cauliflower and broccoli to stir fry for 1 minute. Add the baby corn and sugar to mix thoroughly. Sizzle the wine and ginger juice. Pour in the stock and remaining seasoning. Thicken the sauce with the gravy mix then drop in the sesame oil. Dish and garnish with the carrot pieces.*

葡 汁 四 蔬

Assorted Vegetables in Turmeric Sauce

材料：

白菌 5 安（140克）	糖 1 湯匙
紅蘿蔔 5 安（140克）	菜油 5 湯匙
西蘭花 5 安（140克）	羌 2 片
椰菜花或薯仔 5 安（140克）	葱頭 1 粒
沸水 3 杯	蒜頭 1 粒
鹽 2 湯匙	

調味—鹽 1 茶匙	鮮奶 ½ 杯
糖 ½ 茶匙	椰汁 ½ 杯
酒 1 茶匙	味精 ¼ 茶匙
上湯 ¼ 杯	胡椒粉少許

糭料—麵粉 1 湯匙
黃羗粉 2 湯匙
水 ¼ 杯

製法：

* 白菌修剪妥當洗淨。
* 紅蘿蔔去皮洗淨切成小三角形。
* 西蘭花及椰菜花修妥清洗乾淨，切成小棵。與紅蘿蔔一同放入沸水中加鹽，糖及油 2 湯匙飛水 1 分鐘，撈起過冷河隔乾水份。將白菌亦放於以上鹽水中灼20秒鐘。
* 羗片切絲。葱蒜頭切片。燒紅鑊加油 2 湯匙煮沸，洒鹽 1 茶匙爆香羗，葱，蒜。即傾下四蔬及糖兜炒 1 分鐘，盛起轉放焗盆中。
* 另鑊燒熱加入餘油煮沸，讚酒加上湯，鮮奶及椰汁一起再煮沸。試妥味後，將麵粉，黃羗粉與水搞勻慢慢流入上湯中和成糭汁，淋在四蔬上。
* 將焗盆放入已預熱450度（煤氣8度）之焗爐內。焗約10分鐘，取出熱食。

Ingredients:

5 oz (140 g) fresh mushrooms
5 oz (140 g) carrots
5 oz (140 g) broccoli
5 oz (140 g) cauliflower or potatoes
3 cups boiling water
2 tbsp salt
1 tbsp sugar
5 tbsp corn oil
2 slices ginger
1 shallot
1 garlic clove

Seasoning-
1 tsp salt
½ tsp sugar
1 tsp wine
¼ cup stock
½ cup milk
½ cup coconut milk
¼ tsp M.S.G.
a pinch of pepper

Gravy Mix-
1 tbsp plain flour
2 tbsp turmeric powder
¼ cup water

Method:

* Trim and clean the mushrooms.
* Peel, wash and cut the carrots into wedges.
* Trim, clean and cut the broccoli and cauliflower into small florets.
* Blanch the carrots, broccoli and cauliflower in the boiling water with the salt, sugar and 2 tbsp of oil for 1 minute. Remove, refresh and drain. Scald the mushrooms with the same boiling salted water for 20 seconds.
* Shred the ginger. Slice the shallot and garlic. Heat the wok with 2 tbsp of oil then sprinkle in the 1 tsp salt and sauté the ginger, shallot and garlic. Pour in the mixed vegetables with the sugar to stir fry for 1 minute. Remove and place into a fire proof container.
* Heat another wok with the remaining oil. Sizzle the wine; pour in the stock, milk and coconut milk to bring to the boil. Season to taste. Mix the flour and turmeric powder with the water, then slowly stream into the stock to thicken into a sauce and pour on to the mixed vegetables.
* Place the container into a preheated 450°F (Gas Mark 8) oven to bake for about 10 minutes. Remove and serve hot.

三 元 及 弟
Assorted Vegetables with
White Fungus

材料：

雪耳 1 安（28 克）	調味—酒 1 茶匙
凍水 2 杯	上湯 1 杯
沸水 4 杯	鹽 ½ 茶匙
紅蘿蔔 5 安（140 克）	糖 1 茶匙
佛手瓜（140 克）	生抽 1 茶匙
鹽 2 茶匙	胡椒粉少許
糖 1 茶匙	
菜油 4 湯匙	饁料—生粉 1 茶匙
草菰 5 安（140 克）	水 1 湯匙
薑 2 片	老抽 ¼ 茶匙
葱頭 2 粒	蔴油 1 茶匙
蒜頭 2 粒	

製法：

* 雪耳放凍水中浸 1 小時後修剪妥當，轉放 2 杯沸水中飛水。撈起置水喉下沖凍，置一旁候用。
* 紅蘿蔔及佛手瓜去皮挖成圓球。放入另 2 杯沸水內加鹽、糖及油 1 湯匙飛水 2 分鐘。撈起過冷河。鹽水留起候用。
* 草菰削去蒂後放入以上沸鹽水中飛水，沖洗乾淨，隔乾水份。
* 薑片切絲。葱、蒜頭切片。
* 燒紅鑊加油 2 湯匙煮沸，爆香一半薑絲，葱及蒜片棄去。倒入已隔乾水份之雪耳兜勻。濳酒加上湯 ¼ 杯及部份調味料續煮 1 分鐘，盛在長碟上。
* 另鑊燒紅加入餘油煮沸，洒下鹽爆香其餘薑葱蒜。隨即倒入紅蘿蔔球及佛手瓜球炒勻。濳酒，傾下其餘上湯及調味料文火煮約 1 分鐘。拌入草菰兜勻，即以生粉水埋饁淋在雪耳上即可上桌。

Ingredients:

1 oz (28 g) white fungus
2 cups cold water
4 cups boiling water
5 oz (140 g) carrots
5 oz (140 g) choco or cucumber
2 tsp salt
1 tsp sugar
4 tbsp corn oil
5 oz (140 g) straw mushrooms
2 slices ginger
2 shallots
2 garlic cloves

Seasoning-	Gravy Mix-
1 tsp wine	1 tsp cornflour
1 cup stock	1 tbsp water
½ tsp salt	¼ tsp dark soy
1 tsp sugar	1 tsp sesame oil
1 tsp light soy	
a pinch of pepper	

Method:

* Soak the fungus in the cold water for an hour then trim. Blanch in 2 cups of the boiling water then rinse under a running tap. Leave aside for later use.
* Peel and shape the carrots and choco into small balls. Blanch in the remaining boiling water with the salt, sugar and 1 tbsp of the oil for 2 minutes. Refresh. Leave the salted water for later use.
* Trim and blanch the straw mushrooms in the above salted water and refresh.
* Shred the ginger. Slice the shallots and garlic.
* Heat the wok with 2 tbsp of oil. Sauté half of the ginger, shallot and garlic then discard. Stir in the drained fungus to stir fry thoroughly. Add ¼ cup of the stock and part of the seasoning. Continue to cook for 1 minute then dish.
* Heat another wok with the last tbsp of oil. Sprinkle in the salt to sauté the remaining ginger, shallot and garlic. Pour in the carrots and choco to mix well. Sizzle the wine and add the remaining stock and seasoning. Simmer over low heat for 1 minute. Stir in the straw mushrooms. Thicken the sauce with the gravy mix then scoop over the white fungus and serve.

粉 絲 素 湯

Bean Thread and Vegetables in Soup

材料：

粉絲 2 安（56克）
凍水 2 杯
榨菜 2 安（56克）
紅蘿蔔 2 安（56克）
節瓜或絲瓜 8 安（224克）
油豆腐 10 隻
熟冬菇 4 隻
菜油 2 湯匙
薑 2 片

調味—酒 1 茶匙
　　　上湯 5 杯
　　　鹽 1 茶匙
　　　糖 ½ 茶匙
　　　胡椒粉少許
　　　蔴油 1 茶匙

製法：

* 粉絲浸於凍水中約½小時至軟。撈起剪開置一旁候用。
* 榨菜洗淨切片。紅蘿蔔去皮切花片。
* 節瓜去皮切厚件。油豆腐每個分切兩邊。熟冬菇切片。
* 燒紅鑊加油煮沸爆香薑片。潰酒傾入上湯，冬菇及紅蘿蔔煮 3 分鐘。加入節瓜，榨菜片及油豆腐續煮 2 分鐘。最後將粉絲與調味料一同放入拌勻，盛在湯兜內即可上桌。

Ingredients:

2 oz (56 g) mung bean thread
2 cups cold water
2 oz (56 g) preserved mustard
2 oz (56 g) carrots
8 oz (224 g) courgettes
10 beancurd balls
4 cooked Chinese mushrooms
2 tbsp corn oil
2 slices ginger

Seasoning-
1 tsp wine
5 cups stock
1 tsp salt
½ tsp sugar
a pinch of pepper
1 tsp sesame oil

Method:

* Soak the bean thread in the cold water for half an hour until soft. Cut and leave aside for later use.
* Clean and slice the preserved mustard. Peel, slice and carve the carrots.
* Peel and cut the courgettes into thick pieces. Halve each of the beancurd balls and slice the mushrooms.
* Heat the wok with the oil to sauté the ginger. Sizzle the wine then add the stock, mushrooms and carrots to simmer for 3 minutes. Add the courgettes, preserved mustard and beancurd balls to simmer for another 2 minutes. Stir in the bean thread and seasoning. Remove and serve hot.

螞 蟻 上 樹
Bean Thread with Minced Vegetables

材料：

粉絲 4 安（112克）
凍水 3 杯
炸油½鑊
榨菜 1 安（28克）
紅蘿蔔 1 安（28克）
馬蹄 4 粒
熟冬菇 5 隻
豆腐乾 2 件
青豆¼杯
沸水½杯
菜油 2 湯匙
薑茸½茶匙
葱頭 1 粒切片
紅椒 1 隻切絲

調味—豆瓣醬 2 湯匙
　　　酒 1 茶匙
　　　上湯 1¼杯
　　　生抽 2 茶匙
　　　糖 1 茶匙
　　　蔴油 1 茶匙

製法：

* 粉絲放於凍水中浸透，挑鬆以毛巾吸乾水份分成 3 份。分別放入沸油中炸至鬆起，用吸油紙吸淨餘油候用。
* 榨菜洗淨剁成茸。紅蘿蔔及馬蹄去皮洗淨，與冬菇，豆腐乾一同切幼。
* 青豆放沸水中飛水撈起沖凍隔乾水份。
* 燒紅鑊加油煮沸，爆香薑茸，葱片及紅椒絲。隨即加入雜菜粒兜炒 1 分鐘。將豆瓣醬拌入兜勻。潷酒倒入上湯及調味料，再加粉絲以文火煮約 1 分鐘至水份略乾時灑下青豆及蔴油，即可上桌。

Ingredients:

4 oz (112 g) bean thread
3 cups cold water
½ wok hot oil for deep frying
1 oz (28 g) preserved mustard
1 oz (28 g) carrots
4 water chestnuts
5 cooked Chinese mushrooms
2 pieces spiced beancurd
¼ cup sweet peas
½ cup boiling water
2 tbsp corn oil for sautéeing
½ tsp minced ginger
1 sliced shallot
1 shredded chilli

Seasoning-
2 tbsp broadbean paste
1 tsp wine
1¼ cup stock
2 tsp light soy
1 tsp sugar
1 tsp sesame oil

Method:

* *Soak the bean thread in the cold water; loosen, drain and divide into 3 portions. Deep fry in the hot oil until fluffy. Drain on absorbent kitchen paper.*
* *Wash and mince the preserved mustard. Peel and clean the carrots and water chestnuts. Chop them together with the mushrooms and spicy beancurd finely.*
* *Blanch the sweet peas in the boiling water then refresh and drain.*
* *Heat the wok and bring the oil to the boil. Sauté the ginger, shallot and chilli till fragrant. Stir in the chopped vegetables to fry for 1 minute. Add the hot bean paste to mix well. Sizzle the wine then pour in the stock and seasoning. Mix in the bean thread to simmer for 1 minute until a little stock is left. Garnish with the sweet peas and sprinkle the sesame oil on top. Dish.*

雙 冬 豆 卜

Braised Beancurd Balls with Mushrooms

材料：

冬菇 1 安（28克）
沸水 1 杯
冬瓜或青瓜12安（336克）
豆卜 4 安（112克）
羌 2 片
葱頭 1 粒
蒜頭 1 粒
菜油 3 湯匙

冬菇醃料——鹽¼茶匙
　　　　　糖½茶匙
　　　　　菜油 1 湯匙

調味————鹽¼茶匙
　　　　　酒 1 茶匙
　　　　　上湯½杯
　　　　　生抽 1 茶匙
　　　　　蠔油 1 茶匙
　　　　　糖 1 茶匙
　　　　　胡椒粉少許

饋料————生粉½茶匙
　　　　　水 2 茶匙
　　　　　老抽¼茶匙
　　　　　蔴油 1 茶匙

製法：

* 冬菇洗淨放沸水中浸透，撈起剪去
  蒂，揸乾水份加入醃料略醃後，放
  蒸籠內蒸12分鐘。
* 冬瓜去皮切件候用。
* 豆卜洗淨每個分切爲兩邊。
* 羌片切絲。葱，蒜頭切片。
* 鑊燒紅加油煮沸，洒鹽爆香羌，葱
  ，蒜。傾入冬瓜及豆卜兜炒約 1 分
  鐘。加入冬菇即可潷酒，倒入上湯
  及調味料煮約 2 分鐘。以生粉水埋
  饋加蔴油上碟即成。

Ingredients:

1 oz (28 g) dried Chinese mushrooms
1 cup boiling water
12 oz (336 g) winter melon
　or cucumber
4 oz (112 g) beancurd balls

2 slices ginger
1 shallot
1 garlic clove
3 tbsp corn oil

Mushroom Marinade-
¼ tsp salt
½ tsp sugar
1 tbsp corn oil

Seasoning-
¼ tsp salt
1 tsp wine
½ cup stock
1 tsp light soy
1 tsp oyster sauce
1 tsp sugar
a pinch of pepper

Gravy Mix-
½ tsp cornflour
2 tsp water
¼ tsp dark soy
1 tsp sesame oil

Methods:

* Wash and soak the mushrooms in
  the boiling water then cut off the
  stems. Squeeze out the excess
  water and mix well with the
  marinade. Steam for 12 minutes.
* Peel and cut the winter melon for
  later use.
* Wash and cut the beancurd balls
  into halves.
* Shred the ginger. Slice the shallot
  and garlic.
* Heat the wok till hot to bring the
  oil to the boil. Sprinkle in the salt
  and sauté the ginger, shallot and
  garlic till fragrant. Pour in the
  winter melon and beancurd balls
  to stir fry for 1 minute. Put in the
  mushrooms then sizzle the wine.
  Stir in the stock and seasoning to
  simmer for 2 minutes. Thicken the
  sauce with the gravy mix and drop
  in the sesame oil. Dish and serve.

南 乳 炆 齋

Braised Vegetables with Fermented Beancurd

材料：

熟冬菇 4 安（112 克）
木耳 ½ 安（14 克）
凍水 4 杯
沸水 3 杯
薑 1 片
酒 1 湯匙
髮菜 ½ 安（14 克）
金針 ½ 安（14 克）
粉絲 2 安（56 克）
紅蘿蔔 2 安（56 克）
生菜 4 安（112 克）
炸豆腐 2 安（56 克）
菜油 3 湯匙

調味—南乳 ¼ 杯
　　　酒 1 茶匙
　　　上湯 2 杯
　　　糖 ½ 至 2 湯匙
　　　蔴油 1 湯匙

製法：

* 熟冬菇每隻分切兩邊。
* 木耳放於 2 杯凍水中浸至軟，修剪
  妥當後放入沸水中加薑及酒飛水 1
  分鐘。撈起置水喉下沖凍隔乾水份
  。沸水留作別用。
* 髮菜，金針洗淨剪妥，放入以上沸
  水中飛水，沖淨隔乾水份。
* 粉絲放入餘下凍水中浸約 30 分鐘。
* 紅蘿蔔去皮切片。生菜洗淨。炸豆
  腐切件。
* 燒紅鑊加油煮沸，爆香南乳，冬菇
  及木耳。灒酒倒入上湯再煮 5 分鐘
  。傾下其他材料試妥味續煮 5 分鐘
  ，隨即拌入蔴油及生菜兜勻上碟即
  成。

Ingredients:

*4 oz (112 g) cooked Chinese mush-
  rooms*
½ oz (14 g) black fungus
4 cups water
3 cups boiling water
1 slice ginger
1 tbsp wine
½ oz (14 g) black moss
½ oz (14 g) dried lily bud
2 oz (56 g) mung bean thread
2 oz (56 g) carrots
4 oz (112 g) lettuce
2 oz (56 g) deep fry beancurds
3 tbsp corn oil

Seasoning-
¼ cup fermented beancurd
1 tsp wine
2 cups stock
½ to 2 tbsp sugar
1 tbsp sesame oil

Method:

* *Halve the mushrooms.*
* *Soak the fungus in 2 cups of the
  water till soft. Trim and blanch in
  the boiling water with the ginger
  and wine for 1 minute. Refresh
  and drain. Keep the boiling water
  for later blanching.*
* *Clean and trim the black moss and
  lily bud. Blanch in the above
  boiling water. Rinse and drain.*
* *Soak the bean thread in the
  remaining water for 30 minutes.*
* *Peel and slice the carrots. Wash
  the lettuce and cut the beancurd
  into pieces.*
* *Heat the wok and bring the oil to
  boil. Sauté the fermented beancurd with the mushrooms and
  black fungus. Sizzle the wine and
  pour in the stock to simmer for 5
  minutes. Put in the remaining
  ingredients and season to taste.
  Continue to cook for another 5
  minutes. Add the sesame oil and
  lettuce to mix well. Dish and serve
  hot.*

蚧扒蘭花

Broccoli in Beancurd Sauce

材料：

板豆腐 1 件
沸水 3 杯
西蘭花 12 安（336 克）
鹽水 2 杯
羌 2 片
葱頭 1 粒
菜油 3 湯匙
蛋白 1 隻
紅蘿蔔茸 1 茶匙

調味—鹽 ½ 茶匙
　　　酒 1 茶匙
　　　糖 1 茶匙
　　　上湯 ½ 杯
　　　味精 ¼ 茶匙

饋料—生粉 1 茶匙
　　　水 1 湯匙
　　　蔴油 1 茶匙

製法：

* 板豆腐切細件，放於 1 杯沸水中飛水，撈起隔乾水份候用。
* 西蘭花切成小棵浸於鹽水中片刻。隔去水份後再放入另 2 杯沸水中飛水，撈起置水喉下沖凍。
* 羌，葱頭拍扁。
* 燒紅鑊加油 2 湯匙煮沸，洒鹽爆香羌，葱頭棄去。傾入西蘭花炒約 1 分鐘。潸酒 ½ 茶匙及加糖兜勻盛在碟上。
* 另鑊燒熱加入餘油，潸下餘酒，倒入上湯及豆腐煮沸。放入其餘調味料再以饋料埋饋。隨即拌入蛋白及蔴油，淋在西蘭花上，洒下紅蘿蔔茸即可上碟。

Ingredients:

1 piece soft beancurd
3 cups boiling water
12 oz (336 g) broccoli
2 cups salted water
2 slices ginger
1 shallot
3 tbsp corn oil
1 egg white
1 tsp grated carrot

Seasoning-
½ tsp salt
1 tsp wine
1 tsp sugar
½ cup stock
¼ tsp M.S.G.

Gravy Mix-
1 tsp cornflour
1 tbsp water
1 tsp sesame oil

Methods:

* *Dice the beancurd finely. Blanch in 1 cup of the boiling water and drain for later use.*
* *Cut the broccoli into small sprigs and soak in the salted water. Drain and blanch in the remaining 2 cups of water and rinse under running tap water.*
* *Mash the the ginger and shallot.*
* *Heat the wok with 2 tbsp of the oil to sauté the ginger and shallot then discard. Pour in the broccoli with the salt to fry for a minute. Sizzle in half of the wine and all the sugar. Dish.*
* *Heat another wok with the remaining oil; drop in the remaining wine then pour in the stock. Add the beancurd to bring to the boil. Put in the rest of the seasoning and thicken the sauce with the gravy mix. Stir in the egg white and sesame oil. Pour on to the broccoli and sprinkle the grated carrot on top.*

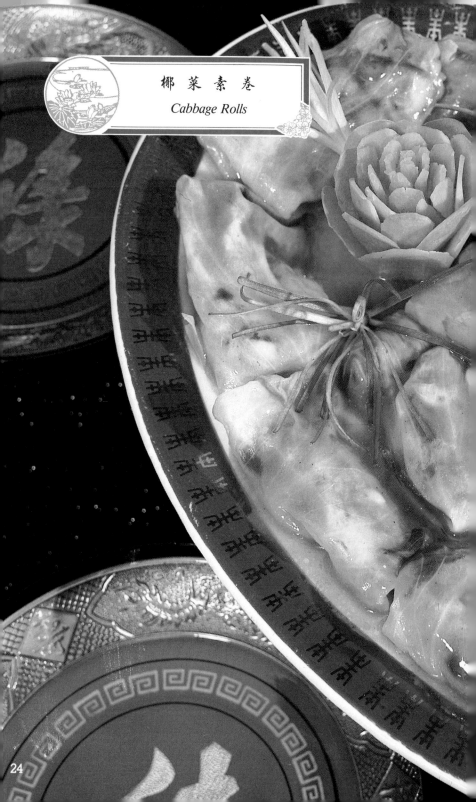

椰菜素卷
Cabbage Rolls

椰 菜 素 卷
Cabbage Rolls

1

4

2

5

3

6

材料：

椰菜葉12塊	調味—酒 2 茶匙
沸水 2 杯	上湯 1 杯
鹽 2 茶匙	鹽 ½ 茶匙
菜油 6 湯匙	糖 1 茶匙
紅蘿蔔 3 安（84克）	蠔油 1 湯匙
草菰 2 安（56克）	胡椒粉少許
白菌 6 粒	
馬蹄 6 粒	饐料—生粉 2 茶匙
熟冬菇 6 隻	水 2 湯匙
麵筋 3 安（84克）	生抽 1 茶匙
銀芽 2 安（56克）	蔴油 1 茶匙

製法：

* 椰菜放於沸水中加鹽及油 2 湯匙飛水至軟身。取出沖淨，以毛巾抹乾水份。鹽水留作別用。
* 紅蘿蔔，草菰及白菌亦放於以上鹽水中飛水。撈起沖凍隔乾水份。
* 馬蹄去皮洗淨與三種菇類，麵筋及紅蘿蔔一同切絲。
* 燒紅鑊加油 2 湯匙煮沸，倒入銀芽及其他材料一同爆炒兜勻。潰酒 1 茶匙加入上湯½杯及調味料煮約 1 分鐘。以一半饐料埋饐。
* 椰菜葉平放桌上，將餡料分作12份。每份餡料放於一塊椰菜葉上捲好。全部椰菜捲妥後，放在碟上轉置蒸籠內猛火蒸 5 分鐘。隔清水份候用。
* 鑊再燒熱加入餘油，潰下其餘酒及上湯試妥味，以餘下饐料流下和成饐淋在菜包上熱食。

Ingredients:

12 cabbage leaves
2 cups boiling water
2 tsp salt
6 tbsp corn oil
3 oz (84 g) carrots
2 oz (56 g) straw mushrooms
6 button mushrooms
6 water chestnuts
6 cooked Chinese mushrooms
3 oz (84 g) gluten rolls
2 oz (56 g) bean sprouts

Seasoning-
2 tsp wine
1 cup stock
½ tsp salt
1 tsp sugar
1 tbsp oyster sauce
a pinch of pepper

Gravy Mix-
2 tsp cornflour
2 tbsp water
1 tsp light soy
1 tsp sesame oil

Methods:

* Blanch the cabbage leaves in the boiling water with the salt and 2 tbsp of the oil until soft. Retain the water, refresh and dry with a towel.
* Blanch the carrots and the straw and button mushrooms in the above boiling salted water. Refresh and drain.
* Peel, wash and shred the water chestnuts together with the mushrooms, gluten rolls and carrots.
* Heat the wok with 2 tbsp of the oil, pour in the bean sprouts and the remaining ingredients to sauté till well mixed. Sprinkle half of the wine then add ½ cup of the stock and seasoning to cook for 1 minute. Thicken the sauce with half of the gravy mix.
* Place the cabbage leaves on to a table. Divide the filling into 12 portions and put 1 portion on to each leaf to wrap up tightly. Arrange on to a platter to steam for 5 minutes over high heat then discard the excess water.
* Reheat the wok with the remaining oil. Sizzle in the rest of the wine and add the remaining stock and seasoning to taste. Thicken the sauce with the remaining gravy mix, stirring constantly until the juice thickens. Pour on to the rolls and serve hot.

北菇菜花

Cauliflower in Brown Sauce

材料：

椰菜花 1 個約 1 磅（½公斤）
鹽水 3 杯
紅蘿蔔花12片
沸水 4 杯
菜油 3 湯匙
鹽 1 茶匙
糖 1 茶匙
味精 1 茶匙
葱頭 1 粒
蒜頭 1 粒
生菜 ½磅（224克）
熟冬菇 2 安（56克）

調味—酒 1 茶匙
　　　生抽 1 茶匙
　　　蠔油 1 湯匙
　　　糖 1 茶匙
　　　胡椒粉少許
　　　水 3 湯匙

饋料—生粉 ½ 茶匙
　　　水 ½ 湯匙
　　　老抽 ¼ 茶匙
　　　蔴油 1 茶匙

製法：

* 椰菜花切小棵，放入鹽水中浸½小時。與紅蘿蔔片一同放入 2 杯沸水中飛水，沖凍隔乾水份候用。

* 另 2 杯沸水放鍋中，加油 1 湯匙，鹽，糖及味精煮沸。將椰菜花放入煨 1 分鐘，撈起置水喉下沖凍。鹽水留起候用。

* 葱，蒜頭切片。生菜洗淨放入以上鹽水中飛水後隔乾盛在碟上。

* 燒紅鑊加入餘油 2 湯匙煮沸，爆香葱，蒜片。倒入椰菜花，紅蘿蔔及冬菇炒透。濽酒加調味料及水兜勻。調妥味後以生粉水和成饋汁，再洒下蔴油即可上碟。

Ingredients:

1 cauliflower, about 1 lb (½ kg)
3 cups salted water for soaking
4 cups boiling water
12 pieces carrot
3 tbsp corn oil
1 tsp salt
1 tsp sugar
1 tsp M.S.G.
1 shallot
1 garlic clove
½ lb (224 g) lettuce
2 oz (56 g) cooked Chinese mush-rooms

Seasoning-
1 tsp wine
1 tsp light soy
1 tbsp oyster sauce
1 tsp sugar
a pinch of pepper
3 tbsp water

Gravy Mix-
½ tsp cornflour
½ tbsp water
¼ tsp dark soy
1 tsp sesame oil

Methods:

* *Section the cauliflower into small florets. Soak in the salted water for 30 minutes. Blanch in 2 cups of the boiling water together with the carrot pieces. Refresh and drain.*
* *Pour 2 cups of the boiling water into a saucepan. Add 1 tbsp of the oil, the salt, sugar and M.S.G. and cook the cauliflower in the water for 1 minute. Rinse under a running tap till cold. Leave the salted water aside for later use.*
* *Slice the shallot and garlic. Wash and blanch the lettuce with the above salted water. Drain and arrange on to a plate.*
* *Heat the wok until hot and bring the remaining oil to the boil. Sauté the shallot and garlic till fragrant. Stir in the cauliflower, carrot and mushrooms to sauté well. Sizzle the wine; add the seasoning and water. Season to taste and thicken the sauce with the gravy mix. Sprinkle the sesame oil and dish.*

嘉饌雜錦

Chopsticks Salad

30

嘉饌雜錦

Chopsticks Salad

1

4

2

5

3

6

材料：

青瓜 1 條約 2 安（56克）
鹽 1 湯匙
紅蘿蔔 1 隻約 2 安（56克）
椰菜 5 安（140克）
沸水 2 杯
酸羌 4 安（112克）
西芹 4 安（112克）
粉皮 4 安（112克）
木耳 ½ 安（14克）
溫水 2 杯
青椒 1 隻
紅椒 1 隻
蒜頭 2 粒
菜油 3 湯匙
銀芽 4 安（112克）

調味—鹽 ⅓ 茶匙　　　　辣油 ½ 茶匙
　　　糖 1 湯匙　　　　　生抽 1 湯匙
　　　蔴醬或花生醬 4 湯匙　上湯 4 湯匙
　　　蔴油 1 茶匙

製法：

* 青瓜去籽切絲。用鹽醃30分鐘。以
  手搾去水份再用毛巾擠乾。
* 紅蘿蔔及椰菜切絲，一同放沸水中
  飛水。酸羌及西芹洗淨亦切絲。
* 粉皮，木耳放溫水中浸30分鐘，隔
  乾水份切絲。青紅椒洗淨去籽皆切
  絲。蒜頭拍扁。
* 燒紅鑊加油 1 湯匙煮沸，爆香蒜頭
  1 粒棄去。倒入銀芽兜炒數秒鐘，
  以碟盛起。
* 調味料放碗中加入上湯和勻調妥味。
* 另鑊燒熱加入餘油 2 湯匙煮沸，爆
  香另 1 粒蒜頭後棄去。除粉皮及銀
  芽外，將全部材料一同放入兜勻，
  盛在長碟上攤凍。將已和勻之調味
  料，粉皮及銀芽倒在雜菜上拌勻即
  成。

Ingredients:

1 cucumber, about 2 oz (56 g)
1 tbsp salt
1 carrot, about 2 oz (56 g)
5 oz (140 g) cabbage
2 cups boiling water
4 oz (112 g) preserved ginger
4 oz (112 g) celery
4 oz (112 g) mung bean sheets
½ oz (14 g) black fungus (optional)
2 cups warm water
1 capsicum
1 chilli
2 garlic cloves
3 tbsp corn oil
4 oz (112 g) bean sprouts

Seasoning-
⅓ tsp salt
1 tbsp sugar
4 tbsp sesame paste or peanut butter
1 tsp sesame oil
½ tsp chilli oil
1 tbsp light soy
4 tbsp stock

Method:

* Deseed and shred the cucumber.
  Marinate with the salt for 30
  minutes. Squeeze out the excess
  water and dry with a towel.
* Shred and blanch the carrot and
  cabbage in the boiling water.
  Wash and shred the preserved
  ginger and celery.
* Soak the mung bean sheets and
  black fungus in the warm water
  for 30 minutes. Drain and shred.
  Wash, deseed and shred the
  capsicum and chilli. Mash the
  garlic.
* Heat the wok with 1 tbsp of the oil
  and sauté 1 of the garlic till
  fragrant, then discard. Pour in the
  bean sprouts to fry for a few
  seconds. Dish.
* Mix the seasoning in a small bowl
  then add the stock to taste.
* Reheat the wok with the remaining oil to sauté the other clove of
  garlic then discard. Stir in all the
  ingredients except the mung bean
  sheets and bean sprouts. Dish and
  leave aside to cool. Pour the mixed
  seasoning, bean sheets and bean
  sprouts on to the vegetables before
  serving.

香 酥 绣 球

Crackling Balls

材料：

豆渣 2 杯
蓮藕茸 2 杯
粟米 1 杯
麵包粒 ½ 杯
青豆 ¼ 杯
熟冬菇粒 ¼ 杯
榨菜粒 2 湯匙
葱粒 1 湯匙
蛋 3 隻打勻
炸油 ½ 鑊

調味—香鹽 1 ½ 茶匙
　　　糖 1 茶匙
　　　生抽 2 茶匙
　　　胡椒粉少許
　　　蔴油 1 茶匙
　　　生粉 3 湯匙
　　　蛋 1 隻

製法：

* 將豆渣，蓮藕茸及粟米同放於大盆中，加入調味料與蛋 1 隻搞勻。
* 麵包粒置已預熱 250 度 (煤氣 ½ 度) 之焗爐內烘乾。
* 將全部材料傾入 (麵包除外) 大盆中混和一起。用手捏成小圓球，沾上打勻之蛋液，放在麵包粒上每個滾上一層外皮。
* 炸油煮沸，將小圓球滑下炸至金黃色。撈起隔去餘油即可上碟。

Ingredients:

2 cups soya bean sediment
2 cups grated lotus root
1 cup creamy sweet corn
½ cup diced bread
¼ cup sweet peas
¼ cup diced cooked Chinese mushrooms
2 tbsp diced preserved mustard
1 tbsp chopped spring onion
3 beaten eggs
½ wok oil for deep frying

Seasoning-
1½ tsp spicy salt
1 tsp sugar
2 tsp light soy
a pinch of pepper
1 tsp sesame oil
3 tbsp cornflour
1 egg

Method:

* *Mix the sediment, lotus root and the sweet corn in a mixing bowl. Add the seasoning and 1 egg to mix thoroughly.*
* *Toast the diced bread in a preheated 250°F (Gas Mark ½) oven until dry.*
* *Stir in all the other ingredients, except the bread, to bind well. Shape into small balls with your hands, then dip in the beaten eggs and coat with the diced bread.*
* *Bring the oil to the boil. Deep fry the balls till golden brown and serve.*

百 花 酥 卷

Crispy Vegetarian Rolls

材料：

餡——腐皮4張　　紅蘿蔔2安（56克）
　　　熟冬菇6隻　　菜油2湯匙
　　　豆腐乾3件　　銀芽6安（168克）
　　　馬蹄12粒　　炸油½鑊

調味——酒1茶匙　　蠔油1茶匙
　　　上湯¼杯　　　糖1茶匙
　　　生抽1湯匙　　胡椒粉少許

饙料——生粉1茶匙
　　　水1湯匙
　　　老抽¼茶匙

脆漿——麵粉2杯　　水1杯
　　　發粉3茶匙　　菜油4湯匙（後下）
　　　生粉4湯匙

製法：

* 腐皮用半濕毛巾抹乾淨，放置一旁
  候用。
* 熟冬菇，豆腐乾，馬蹄及紅蘿蔔皆
  切絲。
* 燒紅鑊加油2湯匙煮沸。放入銀芽
  猛火兜炒8秒鐘。即將其他配料倒
  入拌勻。灒酒加上湯及調味料，調
  妥味後以生粉水埋饙兜勻，盛在碟
  上攤凍。
* 將腐皮平放桌上，用少許饙汁塗在
  上面。再舖上第2層腐皮貼緊。將
  一半餡料放在一邊捲起。兩邊收口
  捲成長條，以繩紮緊。放入蒸籠內
  蒸6分鐘，取出攤凍。
* 麵粉，發粉及生粉同篩在大盆中，
  加水和成漿，放置一旁發30分鐘後
  ，加油再發15分鐘。將腐皮卷放入
  滾滿粉漿，滑下沸油鍋中炸至金黃
  色，撈起切件上碟熱食。

Ingredients:

Filling-
4 beancurd sheets
6 cooked Chinese mushrooms
3 pieces spiced beancurd
12 water chestnuts
2 oz (56g) carrots
2 tbsp corn oil
6 oz (168 g) bean sprouts
½ wok hot oil for deep frying

Seasoning-   Gravy Mix-
1 tsp wine   1 tsp cornflour
¼ cup stock   1 tbsp water
1 tbsp light soy   ¼ tsp dark soy
1 tsp oyster sauce
1 tsp sugar
a pinch of pepper

Batter-
2 cups flour
3 tsp baking powder
4 tbsp cornflour
1 cup water
4 tbsp corn oil, to be added last

Method:

* Wipe the beancurd sheets with a
  wet towel, then leave aside for
  later use.
* Shred the mushrooms, spicy
  beancurd, water chestnuts and
  carrots.
* Heat the wok to bring the oil to the
  boil. Drop in the bean sprouts to
  stir fry for 8 seconds. Add the
  other ingredients to mix well.
  Sprinkle the wine, pour in the
  stock and seasoning. Thicken the
  sauce with the gravy mix and dish.
  Leave aside to cool.
* Place a beancurd sheet flat on the
  table and brush on the gravy
  evenly. Top with the second sheet
  to stick well. Put half of the filling
  on to the sheet and roll up. Tie
  tightly with a string. Repeat. Place
  both of the rolls in the steamer to
  steam for 6 minutes. Take out to
  cool.
* Sift the flour, baking powder and
  cornflour into a mixing bowl. Add
  the water to stir into a batter.
  Leave aside for 30 minutes, then
  blend in the oil and leave aside for
  another 15 minutes. Coat the rolls
  with the batter to deep fry in the
  hot oil until golden brown. Drain
  and cut into pieces then serve hot.

脆 皮 豆 腐
Deep Fried Beancurd

脆 皮 豆 腐
Deep Fried Beancurd

材料：

黃豆 2 磅
水 28 杯
石膏粉 6 茶匙
另水 $\frac{1}{2}$ 杯
菜油 $\frac{1}{2}$ 鑊作炸油用

調味—香鹽 3 湯匙
　　　糖 2 湯匙
　　　胡椒粉 1 茶匙
　　　葱頭斗 2 湯匙

製法：

* 黃豆先用清水蓋面浸 8 至12小時。
　洗淨後隔乾水份。
* 將黃豆放於攪拌機內，逐杯水加入
　磨幼。用密篩隔去豆渣。再倒入紗
　布袋內重揸一次。並須用力壓豆渣
　使能搾出更多豆漿。
* 隔妥之豆漿再加其餘水共成28杯。
　置於深鍋內以文火煮沸。

1

3

2

4

* 石膏粉溶解於另半杯水中。將石膏粉水及豆漿一同冲入大盆內，用毛巾蓋密放置一旁5分鐘使凝結，即成豆花。
* 將12吋丁方之鋼板平放在桌上，架上10吋丁方格。舖上紗布將豆花盛在方格中。紗布覆入蓋面，上放不銹鋼蓋，再加6磅重物壓去水份。約需1小時。
* 移去重物及蓋子，將紗布揭開另用12吋方鋼板一塊蓋着。將豆腐倒置在鋼板上。取去方格及紗布，把豆腐分切成2吋×2吋×1吋（5公分×5公分×2.5公分）厚件。
* 調味料放在碗中和勻，平均洒在每件豆腐上，放置一旁醃30分鐘。將油燒沸，滑入豆腐炸至金黃色，撈起隔去油，即可熱食或留作煮齋用。

Ingredients:

2 lb (1 kg) soya beans
28 cups water
6 tsp plaster of Paris
an extra ½ cup water
½ wok oil for deep frying

Seasoning-
3 tbsp spicy salt
2 tbsp sugar
1 tsp pepper
2 tbsp minced shallot

Special Equipment:

1 sieve
1 muslin bag
1 towel
2 stainless steel sheets measuring 12" × 12"(30 cm²)
a 10" × 10"(25 cm²) bottomless mould
a 20" × 20"(65 cm²) muslin cloth
1 stainless steel lid measuring 9¾" × 9¾"(24 cm²)

Method:

* Soak the beans with enough water to cover them for 8 to 12 hours. Wash and drain.

* Grind the beans in a blender with some of the water. Pour the beans and the water into the blender, 1 cup at a time. Remove the sediments with a sieve then put into the muslin bag and squeeze out as much liquid as possible from the sediments. The liquid is then soya bean milk.

* Add the rest of the water to the soya bean milk to make up to a total of 28 cups. Bring the milk to the boil in a deep saucepan over low heat.

* Dissolve the plaster of Paris in the extra ½ cup of water. Pour the plaster solution and the soya bean milk simultaneously into a large container. Cover with the towel and leave aside to set for 5 minutes. The set liquid is beancurd jelly.

* Place the 12 sq. in. stainless steel sheet on the table top. Put the 10 sq. in. mould on top of the sheet and line it with the muslin cloth. Transfer the half-set jelly into the cloth-lined mould and fold up the cloth to enclosed the beancurd jelly. Add the stainless steel lid on top of the covered jelly and put a 6 lb (3 kg) weight on it in order to press out the excess liquid. Leave aside for an hour.

* Remove the weight and the lid, uncover the beancurd and place the other 12 sq. in. stainless steel sheet on top. Turn the whole mould upside down and remove the square mould and muslin cloth. The set beancurd is now ready to be cut into 2"×2"×1" (5 cm×5 cm×2.5 cm) pieces.

* Mix the seasoning in a bowl and sprinkle evenly on to each beancurd piece then leave aside to marinate for 30 minutes. Bring the oil to the boil then slide the beancurd into the hot oil to deep fry until golden brown. Drain and serve hot.

青 豆 芙 蓉

Deep Fried Egg White
with Peas

材料：

青豆 5 安（140克）
沸水 1 杯
蛋白 8 隻
鹽 ½ 茶匙
胡椒粉 ⅛ 茶匙
炸油 5 杯
菜油 1 湯匙
薑茸 1 茶匙

調味—酒 1 茶匙
　　　上湯 ½ 杯
　　　鹽 ¼ 茶匙
　　　糖 ½ 茶匙

饋料—生粉 ½ 茶匙
　　　水 1 湯匙
　　　蔴油 1 茶匙

製法：

* 青豆放於沸水中飛水片刻。撈起冲凍隔乾水份。
* 蛋白倒入大碗中加鹽及胡椒粉打勻。隨即加青豆拌勻。
* 燒紅鑊倒入炸油 5 杯煮至僅熱，將青豆及蛋白混合物放入鑊中泡至浮起，用罩籬將之撈起隔去除油。放置一旁候用。
* 另鑊燒紅加油 1 湯匙煮沸，爆香薑茸。灒酒加上湯及調味料。以生粉水打饋慢慢流入拌勻。重將蛋料倒入鑊中兜勻，即可上碟。

Ingredients:

5 oz (140 g) sweet peas
1 cup boiling water
8 egg whites
½ tsp salt
1/8 tsp pepper
5 cups corn oil
1 tbsp corn oil for sauteeing
1 tsp minced ginger

Seasoning-
1 tsp wine
½ cup stock
¼ tsp salt
½ tsp sugar

Gravy Mix-
½ tsp cornflour
1 tbsp water
1 tsp sesame oil

Method:

* *Blanch the sweet peas in the boiling water. Refresh and drain.*
* *Whisk the egg whites in a mixing bowl with the salt and pepper, then stir in the sweet peas.*
* *Heat the wok until very hot and pour in the oil to heat until medium warm. Put in the egg mixture to deep fry till it floats. Remove into a strainer to drain off the oil. Leave aside for later use.*
* *Heat another wok with the 1 tbsp of oil and sauté the minced ginger till pungent. Sizzle the wine, add the stock and seasoning. Mix the cornflour with the water then slowly stream into the stock to thicken. Return the egg white into the wok to stir thoroughly. Dish and serve hot.*

炸 生 筋 球

Deep Fried Gluten Balls

材料：

筋粉 2 磅（ 1 公斤 ）
水 2 $\frac{1}{2}$ 杯
發粉 5 茶匙
炸油 $\frac{1}{2}$ 鑊

製法：

* 筋粉篩在桌上開穴，將水傾入慢慢將四週之粉撥入搓成軟糰，放置一旁約20至30分鐘。
* 麵糰重放在桌上連續搓45分鐘至成為一軟韌麵糰，再放置一旁約 1 小時。
* 準備清水一盆，將麵糰放入以手搓洗至粉質溶化，再以另一盆水洗至全無粉質而成為一糰麵筋，即可隔乾水份。
* 麵筋糰與發粉一同搓勻，放置一旁發 6 至 8 小時，取出分切為80小粒。
* 燒紅鑊加油煮沸，將小麵筋粒放入沸油中炸至數倍大，撈起隔淨餘油留作素菜用。

Ingredients:

2 lb (1 kg) high protein flour
2½ cup water
5 tsp baking powder
½ wok oil for deep frying

Method:

* *Sift the flour on to a table and make a well in the centre. Add the water and slowly draw in the flour to knead into a soft dough. Leave aside for 20 to 30 minutes.*
* *Take out the dough to knead continuously for 45 minutes until elastic. Leave aside for 1 hour.*
* *Place the dough in a large bowl of water to wash away the excess flour. Rinse in another bowl of water until a clean dough is left. Drain.*
* *Knead the dough with the baking powder then leave aside to prove for 6 to 8 hours. Cut into 80 equal portions.*
* *Bring the oil to the boil in a wok and deep fry each dough till it has expanded to several times of its original size. Drain and keep for future use.*

素 炸 鮮 奶

Deep Fried Milk Custard

材料：

生粉 2 安（56克）
豆漿 1 $\frac{1}{2}$ 杯
椰汁 $\frac{1}{4}$ 杯
菜油 1 $\frac{1}{2}$ 湯匙
生粉 2 湯匙塗面用
沸炸油 $\frac{1}{2}$ 鍋

調味—酒 $\frac{1}{2}$ 茶匙
　　　鹽 $\frac{1}{2}$ 茶匙
　　　胡椒粉 $\frac{1}{4}$ 茶匙
　　　蔴油 $\frac{1}{2}$ 茶匙

脆漿—麵粉 1 杯
　　　生粉 1 湯匙
　　　發粉 1 茶匙
　　　水 $\frac{1}{2}$ 杯
　　　鹽 $\frac{1}{4}$ 茶匙
　　　菜油 2 湯匙

製法：

* 生粉篩在大碗中，慢慢將 $\frac{1}{2}$ 杯豆漿及全部椰汁拌入搞勻。
* 不銹鋼煲 1 個燒熱，將 1 湯匙油放入煮沸。濽酒傾入其餘 1 杯豆漿煮沸，調妥味即將生粉豆漿慢慢流入搞拌成糊。
* 方或長型糕盆 1 個，將餘下 $\frac{1}{2}$ 湯匙菜油塗在盆內，隨把生粉糊倒入盆中撥平。放置一旁攤凍，轉放雪柜內雪實。
* 麵粉、生粉、發粉同篩在另一大碗中，加入水及鹽一同拌勻。放置一旁發 $\frac{1}{2}$ 小時，將油拌和勻再發 $\frac{1}{2}$ 小時。
* 從雪柜中取出雪實之奶糊，切成小方型。以乾生粉塗勻，轉放入脆漿內裹滿粉漿，放入沸油中炸至金黃色。撈起隔淨油上碟。淮鹽、茄汁跟上。

Ingredients:

2 oz (56 g) cornflour
1½ cups soya bean milk
¼ cup coconut milk
1½ tbsp corn oil
2 tbsp cornflour for dusting
½ wok hot oil for deep frying

Seasoning-
½ tsp wine
½ tsp salt
¼ tsp pepper
½ tsp sesame oil

Coating Batter-
1 cup flour
1 tbsp cornflour
1 tsp baking powder
½ cup water
¼ tsp salt
2 tbsp corn oil

Method:

* *Place the cornflour in a bowl to mix with ½ cup of bean milk and the coconut milk.*
* *Heat a saucepan with 1 tbsp of the oil. Sizzle the wine then bring the remaining bean milk to the boil. Season to taste. Stir in the cornflour and bean milk mix to bind into a paste.*
* *Grease a square tray with the remaining ½ tbsp of oil. Pour in the cornflour paste and leave aside to cool. Chill in the refrigerator for several hours until set.*
* *Sift the flour, cornflour and baking powder into a bowl. Add the water and salt to stir well into a batter. Leave aside to prove for 30 minutes then blend in the oil and leave aside for another 30 minutes.*
* *Remove the milk custard from the refrigerator to cut into squares. Dust with the cornflour then dip in the batter. Deep fry in the hot oil till golden. Drain and serve with spicy salt and tomato ketchcup.*

合 桃 菇 丁
Diced Mushrooms with Walnuts

材料：

合桃肉 4 安（112克）
沸鹽水 2 杯
炸油 3 杯
草菰 3 安（84克）
白菌 3 安（84克）
紅蘿蔔 3 安（84克）
豆腐乾 2 塊
熟冬菇 8 隻
另菜油 2 湯匙
葱頭片 1 粒
蒜頭片 1 粒

調味—鹽 $\frac{1}{4}$ 茶匙
　　　糖 1 茶匙
　　　酒 1 茶匙
　　　素上湯 $\frac{1}{2}$ 杯
　　　生抽 1 茶匙
　　　胡椒粉少許

饎汁—生粉 1 茶匙
　　　水 1 湯匙
　　　老抽 $\frac{1}{4}$ 茶匙
　　　蔴油 1 茶匙

製法：

* 合桃放於沸鹽水中焓約 3 分鐘。取出去衣。沸鹽水留用。
* 鑊燒紅將菜油傾入，立刻將合桃滑下凍油中以文火慢慢浸至油熱而沸，而合桃炸至微黃即可捞起隔油攤凍。
* 將鹽水重煮沸，放入草菰，白菌，紅蘿蔔及豆腐乾煮約 1 分鐘。取出冲水後切粒。熟冬菇亦切粒。
* 另鑊燒紅加油煮沸，洒下鹽爆香葱，蒜片。倒入紅蘿蔔及三種菇粒拌炒 1 分鐘。加豆腐乾粒及糖兜勻。潰酒傾入上湯及其餘調味料煮沸，饎料和勻流下拌勻即可將已炸合桃拌入拋勻上碟。

Ingredients:

4 oz (112 g) shelled walnuts
2 cups boiling salted water
3 cups corn oil for deep frying
3 oz (84 g) straw mushrooms
3 oz (84 g) button mushrooms
3 oz (84 g) carrots
2 pieces spiced beancurd
8 cooked Chinese mushrooms
2 tbsp corn oil for sautéeing
1 sliced shallot
1 sliced garlic

Seasoning-
¼ tsp salt
1 tsp sugar
1 tsp wine
½ cup stock
1 tsp light soy
a pinch of pepper

Gravy Mix-
1 tsp cornflour
1 tbsp water
¼ tsp dark soy
1 tsp sesame oil

Method:

* *Blanch the walnuts in the boiling salted water for 3 minutes then remove the skin. Keep the salted water for later use.*
* *Heat the wok until hot and pour in the oil. Place in the walnuts immediately, while the oil is still cool. Deep fry over low heat until slightly brown. Drain and leave to cool.*
* *Blanch the straw and button mushrooms, carrots and spiced beancurd in the above salted water for 1 minute. Refresh and dice together with the Chinese mushrooms.*
* *Heat the wok again with the 2 tbsp of oil. Sprinkle in the salt then pour in the shallot and garlic to sauté till aromatic. Stir in the carrots and all the mushrooms to fry for 1 minute. Add the spiced beancurd with the sugar to sauté evenly. Sizzle the wine, pour in the stock and seasoning to mix well. Trickle in the gravy mix and sesame oil to thicken the sauce. Stir in the walnuts to toss thoroughly and dish.*

如 意 素 卷

Egg Rolls with Minced Water Chestnut

材料：

餡——馬蹄12安（336克）
　　　西芹2安（56克）
　　　紅蘿蔔1安（28克）
　　　熟冬菇5隻
　　　葱粒2湯匙
　　　榨菜粒1湯匙
　　　蔴油1茶匙
　　　生粉½茶匙

調味——鹽½茶匙　　皮——生粉1茶匙
　　　　糖1茶匙　　　　　鹽¼茶匙
　　　　生抽1茶匙　　　　胡椒粉少許
　　　　胡椒粉少許　　　　蛋2隻
　　　　蔴油½茶匙
　　　　生粉2湯匙

製法：

餡——
* 馬蹄去皮洗淨抹乾，磨爛成茸。西
　芹，紅蘿蔔去皮切幼。熟冬菇亦切
　幼。
* 將馬蹄茸，西芹，紅蘿蔔，冬菇，
　葱粒及榨菜粒全部放在大盆中。拌
　入調味料撻至起膠。
皮——
* 將生粉，鹽及胡椒粉篩在碗中。蛋
　打爛加入拌勻。煎鍋加蔴油燒熱，
　倒入一半蛋料煎成一塊蛋皮。將餘
　下蛋料煎成另一塊蛋皮。
完成——
* 蛋皮平舖在桌上洒上少許生粉。將
　一半餡料平均舖在上面，兩邊向內
　捲起成如意形。再將2條如意卷放
　在塗油蒸籠內蒸8分鐘。取出切片
　熱食。

Ingredients:

Filling-
12 oz (336 g) water chestnuts
2 oz (56 g) celery
1 oz (28 g) carrots
5 cooked Chinese mushrooms
2 tbsp chopped spring onions
1 tbsp chopped preserved mustard
1 tsp sesame oil
½ tsp cornflour

Seasoning-
½ tsp salt
1 tsp sugar
1 tsp light soy
a pinch of pepper
½ tsp sesame oil
2 tbsp cornflour

Pastry:
1 tsp cornflour
¼ tsp salt
a pinch of pepper
2 eggs

Method:

Filling-
* *Peel, clean, dry and grate the water chestnuts into a purée.*
* *Peel and dice the celery and carrots finely. Dice the mushrooms finely.*
* *Place the water chestnut purée, celery, carrots, mushrooms, spring onions and the preserved mustard into a mixing bowl. Stir in the seasoning and pound against the bowl until elastic.*

Pastry-
* *Sift the cornflour, salt and pepper into a mixing bowl then beat in the eggs to mix thoroughly. Heat a frying pan with the sesame oil. Pour in half of the egg batter to cover the bottom of the pan and cook until set. Repeat the process with the other half of the egg batter.*

To Complete-
* *Dust a little cornflour on the egg sheets then spread half of the paste evenly on to it. Roll up into a cylinder or palmier shape. Place the 2 rolls on to a greased plate and cook in a steamer for 8 minutes. Remove, slice and serve hot.*

西 芹 素 鷄

Fried Celery with Mixed Vegetables

材料：

西芹 6 安（168克）
紅蘿蔔 3 安（84克）
沸水 2 杯
鹽 1 茶匙
糖 1 茶匙
味精 ½ 茶匙
菜油 3 湯匙
豆腐乾 4 件
熟冬菇 3 隻
薑 1 片
葱 3 棵
蒜頭 1 粒

調味—鹽 ⅓ 茶匙
　　　酒 1 茶匙
　　　上湯 ¼ 杯
　　　糖 ½ 茶匙
　　　胡椒粉少許

饋料—生粉 1 茶匙
　　　水 1 湯匙
　　　蠔油 1 茶匙
　　　蔴油 1 茶匙

製法：

* 西芹與紅蘿蔔同切成 1 ½ 吋× ¼ 吋
　× ⅛ 吋（3.7 公分× 0.6 公分× 0.3
　公分）幼條，放入沸水中加鹽，
　糖，味精及油 1 湯匙飛水 1 分鐘，
　撈起冲凍隔乾水份。
* 豆腐乾洗淨亦切成與西芹同樣大小
　之幼條。
* 熟冬菇及薑切絲。葱切度。蒜頭切
　片。
* 燒紅鑊加入餘油 2 湯匙煮沸，洒下
　鹽爆香薑，蒜片。倒入西芹，紅蘿
　蔔，豆腐乾及冬菇兜炒約20秒。瓚
　酒加上湯及調味料和勻。以生粉水
　埋饋，洒下葱度拌勻上碟。

Ingredients:

6 oz (168 g) celery
3 oz (84 g) carrots
2 cups boiling water
1 tsp salt
1 tsp sugar
½ tsp M.S.G.
3 tbsp corn oil
4 pieces spiced beancurd
3 cooked Chinese mushrooms
1 slice ginger
3 spring onions
1 garlic clove

Seasoning-
⅓ tsp salt
1 tsp wine
¼ cup stock
½ tsp sugar
a pinch of pepper

Gravy Mix-
1 tsp cornflour
1 tbsp water
1 tsp oyster sauce
1 tsp sesame oil

Method:

* *Cut the celery and carrots into 1½" × ¼" × 1/8" (3.7 cm × 0.6 cm × 0.3 cm) pieces. Blanch in the boiling water with the salt, sugar, M.S.G. and 1 tbsp of oil for 1 minute. Refresh and drain.*
* *Wash and cut the spiced beancurd into the same size as the celery.*
* *Shred the mushrooms and the ginger. Section the spring onions. Slice the garlic.*
* *Heat the wok with the remaining oil and sprinkle the salt to sauté the ginger and garlic till aromatic. Put in the celery, carrots, beancurd and mushrooms to stir fry for 20 seconds. Sizzle the wine, add the stock and seasoning. Thicken the sauce with the gravy mix. Scatter the spring onions on top and dish.*

菠蘿炒飯

Fried Rice with Diced Pineapple

材料：

大菠蘿 1 個
鹽水 2 杯
凍飯 2 杯
蛋 1 隻
鹽少許
胡椒粉少許
青豆 $\frac{1}{4}$ 杯
沸水 $\frac{1}{2}$ 杯
糖羗 $\frac{1}{2}$ 安（14克）
熟冬菇 3 隻
菜油 2 湯匙
葱粒 1 湯匙

調味—生抽 1 $\frac{1}{2}$ 湯匙
　　　胡椒粉少許
　　　蔴油 1 茶匙

製法：

* 菠蘿在頂部距離 2 吋（5 公分）左右切開成一個蓋。菠蘿身以利刀挖出果肉後，留作盛器。
* 將菠蘿肉用鹽水略浸洗淨抹乾。將 $\frac{1}{2}$ 杯份量之菠蘿肉切成丁。其餘留作別用。
* 凍飯取出弄散，放在碟上候用。
* 蛋打爛加鹽及胡椒粉打勻。
* 青豆放於沸水中飛水後。置水喉下沖凍隔乾候用。
* 糖羗與熟冬菇皆切粒。
* 燒紅鑊加油煮沸，將蛋液倒入略炒後即加入白飯同炒約 1 分鐘。隨將其餘材料傾入兜勻。調妥味洒下葱粒再炒十數下。將熱飯倒入菠蘿窩上即可上桌。

Ingredients:

1 large pineapple
2 cups salted water
2 cups cold cooked rice
1 egg
a pinch of salt
a pinch of pepper
¼ cup sweet peas
½ cup boiling water
½ oz (14 g) candied ginger
3 cooked Chinese mushrooms
2 tbsp corn oil
1 tbsp chopped spring onion

Seasoning-
1½ tbsp light soy
a pinch of pepper
1 tsp sesame oil

Method:

* *Slice off the cap of the pineapple 2" (5 cm) from the top and remove the flesh to make a container with a lid.*
* *Rinse the pineapple flesh with the salted water and towel dry. Dice enough pineapple to make up half a cup of fruit. Store away the rest for other usage.*
* *Separate the cold cooked rice into individual grains and place in a plate for later use.*
* *Beat the egg with the salt and pepper.*
* *Blanch the sweet peas in the boiling water and refresh under a running tap. Drain.*
* *Dice the ginger and mushrooms.*
* *Heat the wok to bring the oil to the boil. Scramble the egg then stir in the rice to fry for a minute. Add the remaining ingredients and season to taste. Sprinkle the spring onion to toss well and scoop into the pineapple shell to serve hot.*

腐 皮 糯 卷

Glutinous Rice in Beancurd Rolls

材料：

榨菜 1 安（28克）
豆腐乾 2 件
紅蘿蔔 2 安（56克）
熟冬菇 2 安（56克）
鹹蛋黃 6 隻
菜油 2 湯匙
糯米飯 4 杯
腐皮 3 塊
芫茜茸 1 湯匙
生粉 2 茶匙
　＋水 1½湯匙
炸油½鑊

調味—生抽 1 湯匙
　　　老抽 1 湯匙
　　　糖 1 湯匙
　　　味精¼茶匙
　　　菜油 2 湯匙
　　　胡椒粉少許

製法：

* 榨菜，豆腐乾，紅蘿蔔及熟冬菇洗
  淨皆切粒。
* 鹹蛋黃每隻分切四份。
* 燒紅鑊加油煮沸，放入榨菜，豆腐
  乾，紅蘿蔔及冬菇爆炒片刻。將糯
  米飯加入和勻，再加調味拌妥。
* 將每塊腐皮以濕毛巾略抹後，對摺
  成一半，舖一層糯米飯在直邊上，
  上面排放一行鹹蛋黃及芫茜茸，再
  以另一層糯米飯蓋之。將腐皮慢慢
  覆入捲成粗條，以生粉水埋口。
* 將腐皮卷滑入沸滾之炸油中炸至金
  黃色後切片。或放蒸籠內蒸10分鐘
  後切件再炸上碟。

Ingredients:

1 oz (28 g) preserved mustard
2 pieces spiced beancurd
2 oz (56 g) carrots
*2 oz (56 g) cooked Chinese mush-
  rooms*
6 salted egg yolks
2 tbsp corn oil
4 cups cooked glutinous rice
3 beancurd sheets
1 tbsp chopped parsley
2 tsp cornflour + 1½ tbsp water
½ wok oil for deep frying

Seasoning-
1 tbsp light soy
1 tbsp dark soy
1 tbsp sugar
¼ tsp M.S.G.
2 tbsp corn oil
a pinch of pepper

Method:

* *Wash and dice the mustard, beancurd, carrots and mushrooms into
  very small pieces.*
* *Cut the egg yolks into quarters.*
* *Heat the wok and add the oil to
  stir fry the mustard, beancurd,
  carrots and the mushrooms. Add
  the glutinous rice and seasoning to
  mix well.*
* *Wipe the beancurd sheets with the
  wet towel and fold each sheet into
  half. Place a layer of the rice along
  the straight edge, arrange a row of
  egg yolk and chopped parsley on
  top and cover with another layer
  of the rice. Wrap and roll up to
  form a cylinder. Seal with the
  cornflour and water mix.*
* *Heat the wok and bring the oil to
  boil. Deep fry each roll until
  golden brown. Cut into smaller
  pieces to serve. Alternatively,
  steam for 10 minutes then slice
  and deep fry in the hot oil to serve.*

羅 漢 上 素
Lo Hon Chai

材料：

白果10粒
紅蘿蔔 2 安（56克）
冬笋 2 安（56克）
西蘭花 4 安（112克）
草菇10隻
白菌10隻
油筋10個
沸水 4 杯

雪耳 $\frac{1}{2}$ 安
凍水 2 杯
羗汁 1 茶匙
酒 1 茶匙
菜油 3 湯匙
銀芽 4 安（112克）
熟冬菇10隻

調味—鹽½茶匙
　　　酒 1 茶匙
　　　上湯½杯
　　　生抽 1 茶匙
　　　糖 1 茶匙

饆料—生粉 1 茶匙
　　　水 1 湯匙
　　　老抽¼茶匙
　　　蔴油 1 茶匙

製法：

* 白果去殼去衣。紅蘿蔔及冬筍去皮切片。西蘭花切成小段。
* 草菇，白菌洗淨削去蒂，連同白果，紅蘿蔔，冬筍，西蘭花及油筋放於 3 杯沸水中飛水，過冷河後隔乾。將每個油筋分切為兩邊。
* 雪耳用凍水浸透剪去蒂，以其餘一杯沸水加羌汁，酒煮片刻。隔乾候用。
* 燒紅鑊加油 1 湯匙煮沸爆炒銀芽約數秒鐘。盛起候用。
* 將鑊再燒紅，加入餘油 2 湯匙煮沸。洒鹽傾入白果，紅蘿蔔，冬筍，西蘭花，草菇，白菌及雪耳猛火炒½分鐘。潛酒加上湯及調妥味。
* 將冬菇，銀芽傾入鑊中兜勻，以生粉水加老抽埋饆。洒下蔴油即可上碟。

Ingredients:

10 ginkgo nuts
2 oz (56 g) carrots
2 oz (56 g) bamboo shoots
4 oz (112 g) broccoli
10 straw mushrooms
10 button mushrooms
10 deep-fried gluten balls
4 cups boiling water
½ oz (14 g) white fungus
2 cups water
1 tsp ginger juice
1 tsp wine
3 tbsp corn oil
4 oz (112 g) bean sprouts
10 cooked Chinese mushrooms

Seasoning-
½ tsp salt
1 tsp wine
½ cup stock
1 tsp light soy
1 tsp sugar

Gravy Mix-
1 tsp cornflour
1 tbsp water
¼ tsp dark soy
1 tsp sesame oil

Mehtod:

* Shell and skin the ginkgo nuts. Peel and slice the carrots and bamboo shoots. Cut the broccoli into small sprigs.
* Trim and clean the straw and button mushrooms. Blanch the ginkgo nuts, carrots, bamboo shoots, broccoli, straw and button mushrooms and the gluten balls in 3 cups of the boiling water. Refresh and drain. Cut the gluten balls into halves.
* Soak the white fungus in the water and trim. Parboil in the remaining cup of boiling water together with the ginger juice and wine for a minute. Refresh and drain.
* Heat the wok with 1 tbsp of the oil to sauté the bean sprouts over high heat for a few seconds. Dish.
* Reheat the wok till very hot, add the remaining oil and bring to the boil. Sprinkle in the salt and sauté the ginkgo nuts, carrots, bamboo shoots, broccoli, straw and button mushrooms and the white fungus to fry for half a minute. Sizzle the wine, add the stock and season to taste.
* Pour in the Chinese mushrooms and bean sprouts to toss thoroughly. Thicken the sauce with the gravy mix and the dark soy. Drop in the sesame oil and dish.

炒芽菜崧

Minced Soya Bean Sprouts with Assorted Vegetables

材料：

大豆芽10安（280克）
豆腐乾 2 件
榨菜 2 安（56克）
草菇 2 安（56克）
西芹 4 安（112克）
熟冬菇 4 隻
葱頭 1 粒
菜油 2 湯匙
紅蘿蔔茸 4 湯匙
馬蹄茸 3 湯匙
葱粒 2 湯匙
脆合桃茸¼杯

調味—鹽¼茶匙
　　　酒 1 茶匙
　　　上湯½杯
　　　生抽 1 茶匙
　　　蠔油 1 茶匙
　　　糖 1 茶匙
　　　胡椒粉少許

饋料—生粉 1 茶匙
　　　水 1 湯匙
　　　老抽½茶匙

製法：

* 大豆芽摘好洗淨剁碎，放於白鑊中文火焗乾。
* 豆腐乾，榨菜，草菇，西芹及熟冬菇全部洗淨皆切幼。葱頭剁碎。
* 燒紅鑊加油煮沸,洒下鹽爆香葱頭棄去。傾入全部配料（葱粒及合桃茸除外）炒勻。灒酒加上湯及調味兜勻。即以生粉水加老抽流入埋饋。最後洒葱粒及合桃茸上碟。

Ingredients:

10 oz (280 g) soya bean sprouts
2 pieces spiced beancurd
2 oz (56 g) pickled mustard
2 oz (56 g) straw mushrooms
4 oz (112 g) celery or choco
4 cooked Chinese mushrooms
1 shallot
2 tbsp corn oil
4 tbsp minced carrots
3 tbsp minced water chestnuts
2 tbsp chopped spring onion
¼ cup chopped toasted walnuts

Seasoning-
¼ tsp salt
1 tsp wine
½ cup stock
1 tsp light soy
1 tsp oyster sauce
1 tsp sugar
a pinch of pepper

Gravy Mix-
1 tsp cornflour
1 tbsp water
½ tsp dark soy

Method:

* *Clean, trim and chop the bean sprouts. Parch in a dry hot wok over low heat.*
* *Wash and chop the spiced beancurd, pickled mustard, straw mushrooms, celery and the Chinese mushrooms into small pieces. Mince the shallot.*
* *Heat the wok with the oil and sprinkle in the salt to sauté the shallot till fragrant. Pour in all the ingredients except the spring onion and walnuts. Stir fry thoroughly. Sizzle the wine, add the stock and seasoning to mix well. Drop in the gravy mix to thicken the sauce. Scatter the spring onion and walnuts on top and dish.*

酥 炸 素 肉

Mixed Vegetable Crisps

材料：

馬蹄 8 粒
板豆腐 1 磅（½ 公斤）
豆腐乾 2 件
榨菜 1 安（28克）
葱 2 棵
芫茜 ¼ 安（ 7 克）
熟冬菇 2 安（56克）
腐皮 3 塊
生粉 ½ 杯＋水 ¼ 杯
炸油 ½ 鑊

調味——鹽 ½ 茶匙
　　　糖 1 茶匙
　　　生抽 1 茶匙
　　　胡椒粉少許
　　　蔴油 ½ 茶匙
　　　生粉 2 湯匙

製法：

* 馬蹄去皮磨爛成茸放於大盆中。
* 板豆腐搓爛放入盆中。將調味料拌勻試妥味。
* 豆腐乾，榨菜，葱，芫茜及冬菇全部洗淨切碎後亦放在大盆中，加入調味料撻透。
* 腐皮每張切爲 2 塊，以生粉加水塗在上面。將兩片腐皮貼緊，餡料平舖在一邊，以另一邊腐皮蓋在上面。邊沿以生粉漿貼牢，使成爲三角形。
* 炸油燒沸，將火轉慢少許後。把三角形腐皮包放入炸至金黃色。撈起切小件上碟。

Ingredients:

8 water chestnuts
1 lb (½ kg) soft beancurds
2 pieces spiced beancurd
1 oz (28 g) preserved mustard
2 spring onions
¼ oz (7 g) parsley
2 oz (56 g) cooked Chinese
  mushrooms
3 beancurd sheets
½ cup cornflour + ¼ cup water
½ wok oil for deep frying

Seasoning-
½ tsp salt
1 tsp sugar
1 tsp light soy
a pinch of pepper
½ tsp sesame oil
2 tbsp cornflour

Method:

* Peel and grate the water chestnuts and put into a mixing bowl.
* Mash the soft beancurd. Mix the seasoning thoroughly in a small bowl and adjust the flavour according to taste.
* Wash and chop the spiced beancurd, preserved mustard, spring onions, parsley and mushrooms. Put these ingredients into the mixing bowl and stir in the mixed seasoning to pound the mixture until firm.
* Cut each beancurd sheet into halves and stick them together with the cornflour and water mix. Place a thin layer of filling on one side and cover with other side to form a triangle. Seal with the cornflour mix. Repeat the process until the beancurd sheets are used up.
* Heat the wok and bring the oil to the boil. Deep fry the triangles over moderate heat till golden brown. Drain and cut into serving pieces.

金 錢 遍 地
Mushrooms in Oyster Sauce

材料：

冬菇仔 4 安（112克）　菜油 4 湯匙
沸水 4 杯　　　　　　 紅蘿蔔 4 安（112克）
生菜½磅（224克）　　 羗 2 片
鹽 1 湯匙　　　　　　 葱頭 1 粒
糖 1 茶匙　　　　　　 蒜頭 1 粒

冬菇醃料—鹽½茶匙
　　　　　糖 1 茶匙
　　　　　菜油 1½湯匙

調味———酒 1 茶匙
　　　　　冬菇水½杯
　　　　　蠔油 1 湯匙
　　　　　糖½茶匙

饂料———生粉 1 茶匙
　　　　　水 1 湯匙
　　　　　老抽¼茶匙
　　　　　蔴油 1 茶匙

製法：

* 冬菇洗淨去蒂，放於 2 杯沸水中浸
  至軟撈起。冬菇水留作上湯用。將
  冬菇放入醃料中撈勻以中火蒸12至
  15分鐘。
* 生菜洗淨，放入餘下之沸水中加鹽
  ，糖及油 2 湯匙灼半分鐘撈起。隔
  乾水份後排放碟中。鹽水留起別用
  。
* 紅蘿蔔切花，用以上鹽水飛水後冲
  凍隔乾。羗，葱，蒜頭拍扁。
* 燒紅鑊加入餘油 2 湯匙煮沸，放入
  羗，葱，蒜爆香棄去，倒下冬菇及
  紅蘿蔔兜炒約 1 分鐘。潷酒加冬菇
  上湯及調味料續煮 1 分鐘。以生粉
  水加老抽埋饂，盛在生菜上即可上
  桌。

Ingredients:

4 oz (112 g) dried Chinese mush-rooms
4 cups boiling water
½ lb (224 g) lettuce
1 tbsp salt
1 tsp sugar
4 tbsp corn oil
4 oz (112 g) carrots
2 slices ginger
1 shallot
1 garlic clove

Mushroom Marinade-
½ tsp salt
1 tsp sugar
1½ tbsp corn oil

Seasoning-
1 tsp wine
½ cup mushroom stock
1 tbsp oyster sauce
½ tsp sugar

Gravy Mix-
1 tsp cornflour
1 tbsp water
¼ tsp dark soy
1 tsp sesame oil

Method:

* *Wash and remove the stalks of the mushrooms. Soak in 2 cups of the boiling water until soft. Squeeze out the water and reserve as stock. Mix the mushrooms with the marinade and steam for 12 to 15 minutes over moderate heat.*
* *Wash the lettuce. Bring the remaining boiling water to the boil together with the salt, sugar and 2 tbsp of the oil and blanch the lettuce for half a minute. Drain and dish. Keep the salted water for later use.*
* *Slice and carve the carrots. Blanch in the same boiling salted water, rinse and drain. Mash the ginger, shallot and garlic.*
* *Heat the wok with the remaining oil to sauté the ginger, shallot and garlic till aromatic then discard. Put in the mushrooms and carrots to stir fry for 1 minute. Sizzle the wine then pour in the mushroom stock and seasoning. Continue to cook for 1 minute then thicken the sauce with the gravy mix. Scoop on to the lettuce and serve.*

粟 米 蝦 丸
Potato Balls in
Sweet Corn Sauce

材料：

粟米 1 杯
薯仔 8 安（224克）
沸水 3 杯
紅蘿蔔茸 $\frac{1}{4}$ 杯
馬蹄茸 $\frac{1}{4}$ 杯
葱粒 2 湯匙

生粉 $\frac{1}{4}$ 杯
炸油 5 杯
蒜頭 1 粒
芫茜 1 棵
菜油 2 湯匙

醃料—鹽 ½ 茶匙
　　　糖 1 茶匙
　　　生抽 1 茶匙
　　　生粉 1 湯匙
　　　蔴油 1 茶匙

調味—酒 1 茶匙
　　　上湯 ½ 杯
　　　糖 ½ 茶匙
　　　胡椒粉少許

饋料—生粉 1 茶匙
　　　水 1 湯匙
　　　蔴油 1 茶匙

製法：

* 粟米盛於碗中，放置一旁候用。
* 薯仔洗淨置沸水中炻熟。撕去皮按爛成茸。
* 將薯茸，紅蘿蔔茸，馬蹄茸及葱粒全部放於深盆內，加入醃料搞成薯泥。以手唧成小丸子後塗上生粉。
* 鑊燒紅傾入炸油煮沸，將小丸子放入炸至金黃色，撈起隔淨油。
* 蒜頭剁茸。芫茜洗淨摘妥。
* 鑊再燒紅加油煮沸，爆香蒜茸。濽酒加上湯，倒入粟米，薯丸及調味料煮 1 分鐘。以生粉水慢慢流入埋饋上碟，芫茜洒在上面。

Ingredients:

1 cup creamy sweet corn
8 oz (224 g) potatoes
3 cups boiling water
¼ cup grated carrots
¼ cup grated water chestnuts
2 tbsp chopped spring onions
¼ cup cornflour
5 cups oil for deep frying
1 garlic clove
1 parsley sprig
2 tbsp corn oil

Marinade-
½ tsp salt
1 tsp sugar
1 tsp light soy
1 tbsp cornflour
1 tsp sesame oil

Seasoning-
1 tsp wine
½ cup stock
½ tsp sugar
a pinch of pepper

Gravy Mix-
1 tsp cornflour
1 tbsp water
1 tsp sesame oil

Method:

* Put the sweet corn in a bowl and leave aside for later use.
* Wash and cook the potatoes in the boiling water. Peel and mash into a purée.
* Place the potato purée, carrots, water chestnuts and spring onions in a mixing bowl. Add the marinade to mix into a paste. Shape into small balls then dust with the cornflour.
* Bring the oil to the boil in a wok and put in the potato balls to deep fry till golden brown. Drain.
* Mince the garlic. Wash and trim the parsley.
* Heat the 2 tbsp oil in the wok to sauté the garlic. Sizzle the wine and add the stock to bring to the boil, then put in the sweet corn, potato balls and seasoning to cook for a minute. Slowly blend in the gravy mix to thicken into a sauce. Sprinkle the parsley on top and dish.

鵪蛋冬菇

Quails' Eggs in Mushrooms

材料：

冬菇20隻
沸水 2 杯
鵪蛋20隻
青豆20粒
蔥頭 1 粒
蒜頭 1 粒
菜油 2 湯匙

冬菇醃料——鹽¼茶匙
　　　　　糖 1 茶匙
　　　　　菜油 1 湯匙

調味————酒 1 茶匙
　　　　　冬菇上湯½杯
　　　　　生抽 2 茶匙
　　　　　糖 1 茶匙
　　　　　蠔油 1 茶匙
　　　　　胡椒粉少許

饡料————生粉 1 茶匙
　　　　　水 1 湯匙
　　　　　蔴油 1 茶匙

製法：

* 冬菇洗淨，放於 2 杯沸水中浸透。
  揸出水份留作上湯用。將醃料加入
  冬菇中撈勻，放蒸籠內蒸12分鐘，
  取出放置一旁候用。
* 將冬菇反轉平放碟上，以手指將冬
  菇內部按扁。鵪蛋去壳，每隻冬菇
  內放下一隻鵪蛋，蛋上各放一粒青
  豆。重放蒸籠內蒸約 3 分鐘。
* 蔥，蒜頭去皮洗淨拍扁。
* 燒紅鑊加油煮沸，放入蔥，蒜頭炸
  香棄去。潷酒加冬菇上湯再煮滾。
  調妥味以生粉水打饡，洒下蔴油淋
  在冬菇上即成。

Ingredients:

20 Chinese mushrooms
2 cups boiling water
20 quails' eggs
20 sweet peas
1 shallot
1 garlic clove
2 tbsp corn oil

Mushroom Marinade-
¼ tsp salt
1 tsp sugar
1 tbsp corn oil

Seasoning-
1 tsp wine
½ cup mushroom stock
2 tsp light soy
1 tsp sugar
1 tsp oyster sauce
a pinch of pepper

Gravy Mix-
1 tsp cornflour
1 tbsp water
1 tsp sesame oil

Method:

* *Clean and soak the mushrooms in the boiling water, then trim. Squeeze out the excess water and retain as stock. Mix the mushrooms with the marinade and place in a steamer to cook for 12 minutes. Remove and leave aside for later use.*
* *Place the mushrooms upside down on a platter and then press the inside with your finger. Shell the quails' eggs then arrange one in each mushroom and top with 1 sweet pea. Return into the steamer to steam for 3 minutes.*
* *Peel, wash and mash the shallot and garlic.*
* *Heat the wok with the oil and sauté the shallot and garlic till aromatic then discard. Sizzle the wine and add the stock to bring to the boil. Season to taste. Mix the cornflour with the water and stream in to the sauce to thicken. Drop in the sesame oil then pour on to the mushrooms. Serve hot.*

粟 米 會 飯

Rice with Sweet Corn Sauce

材料：

熱飯 3 杯
豆腐乾 2 件
菜油 2 湯匙
葱頭 1 粒拍扁
粟米 1 杯
蛋 1 隻打勻

調味—酒 1 茶匙
　　　上湯 ½ 杯
　　　鹽 ¼ 茶匙
　　　糖 ½ 茶匙
　　　味精 ⅛ 茶匙
　　　胡椒粉少許

饂料—生粉 1 茶匙
　　　水 1 湯匙
　　　蔴油 1 茶匙

製法：

* 熱飯以竹筷子挑鬆，仍放電飯煲中維持溫暖。
* 豆腐乾片去皮洗淨切幼粒，放置一旁候用。
* 燒紅鑊加油煮沸，爆香葱頭棄去。潷酒加上湯再煮沸。隨即傾入粟米及豆腐乾粒煮 1 分鐘。調味料拌勻加入，試至合味。
* 將生粉與水和勻流入煮成饂汁，再加蛋液與蔴油拌勻。
* 熱飯盛放在熱碟中，將粟米淋在上面即可。

Ingredients:

3 cups hot cooked rice
2 pieces spiced beancurd
2 tbsp corn oil
1 mashed shallot
1 cup creamy sweet corn
1 beaten egg

Seasoning-
1 tsp wine
½ cup stock
¼ tsp salt
½ tsp sugar
⅛ tsp M.S.G.
a pinch of pepper

Gravy Mix-
1 tsp cornflour
1 tbsp water
1 tsp sesame oil

Method:

* *Loosen the cooked rice with a pair of chopsticks, then leave in the rice cooker to keep warm.*
* *Peel, wash and dice the spiced beancurd. Leave aside for later use.*
* *Bring the oil to the boil in the wok. Sauté and discard the shallot. Sizzle the wine and add the stock to bring to the boil. Pour in the sweet corn and the spiced bean-curd to simmer for a minute. Season to taste.*
* *Mix the cornflour with the water then trickle into the boiling solution to thicken into a sauce. Stir in the beaten egg with the sesame oil.*
* *Dish the hot cooked rice on to a hot platter. Pour the sweet corn sauce on top and serve hot.*

美味豆花

Savoury Beancurd Jelly

材料：

黃豆 8 安（224克）　調味—生抽½杯
水13杯　　　　　　　糖 2 湯匙
石膏粉 1½茶匙　　　　熟油 2 湯匙
粟粉½安（14克）
另水½杯

配料—熟冬菇 6 隻
　　　馬蹄 4 粒
　　　榨菜 2 安（56克）
　　　西芹 2 安（56克）
　　　甘筍 2 安（56克）
　　　菜油 2 湯匙起鑊

製法：

* 黃豆洗淨以清水蓋過浸着。夏天需浸 8 小時而冬天則需12小時。將豆沖洗乾淨隔乾水份。
* 黃豆倒入搞拌器內加水 3 杯，以中等速度打約40秒鐘使成漿，以篩將豆渣隔去。轉放紗布袋中再加水 2 杯重搾一次，便成豆漿。
* 豆漿內再加其餘水合共有13杯流質。
* 將豆漿倒在深鍋內以慢火煮沸至泡沫升近鍋邊時即立刻停火。
* 石膏粉，粟粉及另½杯水一同放在碗中拌勻。與沸豆漿同時快速沖入大盆中蓋以毛巾，放置一旁10分鐘使凝結成豆腐花。
* 將熟冬菇及其餘配料皆切成幼粒，燒紅鑊加油 2 湯匙爆香各粒粒，倒在豆腐花上。
* 生抽以文火煮沸加糖煮溶後再拌入熟油淋在豆腐花上熱食。

Ingredients:

8 oz (224 g) soya beans
13 cups water
1½ tsp plaster of Paris
½ oz (14 g) cornflour
extra ½ cup water

Topping-
6 cooked mushrooms
4 water chestnuts
2 oz (56 g) preserved mustard
2 oz (56 g) celery
2 oz (56 g) carrots
2 tbsp corn oil for sautéeing

Seasoning-
½ cup light soy
2 tbsp sugar
2 tbsp cooked corn oil

Method:

* Wash and soak the soya beans in enough water for 8 hours in the summer and 12 hours in the winter. Rinse the beans under tap water then drain.
* Pour the beans into a blender with 3 cups of the water and blend on maximum speed for 40 seconds to grind into a purée. Remove the sediments with a fine sieve, then put into the muslin bag and squeeze out as much liquid as possible from the sediments. Add 2 more cups of water to repeat the procedure. The liquid is soya bean milk.
* Add the remaining cups of water to make up to 13 cups of soya bean milk.
* Pour the bean milk in a saucepan to bring to boil over low heat till it froths up near the edge of the saucepan. Quickly turn the fire off.
* Dissolve the plaster of Paris and cornflour in a bowl with the extra water. Pour the bean milk and plaster solution rapidly together into a container. Cover with a big towel. Leave aside for 10 minutes to set. The set liquid is the bean-curd jelly.
* Dice the cooked mushrooms and all the other ingredients. Heat the wok with 2 tbsp oil to sauté all the diced ingredients till aromatic. Scoop over the soya bean jelly.
* Bring the light soy to the boil over lower heat then pour in the sugar to simmer till dissolved. Add the cooked oil to stir well and place on top of the jelly. Serve hot.

雪 菜 三 絲

Shredded Vegetable Combination

材料：

雪菜 4 安（112克）
鹽水 2 杯
紅蘿蔔 4 安（112克）
笋或椰菜 4 安（112克）
沸水 2 杯
熟冬菇 6 隻
葱 2 棵
蒜頭 1 粒
菜油 3 湯匙

調味—糖 2 茶匙
　　　酒 1 茶匙
　　　上湯 ¼ 杯
　　　生抽 2 茶匙
　　　胡椒粉少許

饡料—生粉 ½ 茶匙
　　　水 ½ 湯匙
　　　老抽 ¼ 茶匙
　　　麻油 1 茶匙

製法：

* 雪菜預早浸在鹽水中 2 小時。撈起
  沖洗乾淨後，切成 1 吋（2.5 公分）
  度，置白鑊中文火烙乾。
* 紅蘿蔔及笋去皮切成與雪菜同樣大
  小。以 2 杯沸水煮½分鐘飛水。倒
  起隔乾水份。
* 冬菇切絲。葱洗淨切度。蒜頭切片。
* 燒紅鑊加油爆香蒜片。隨將雪菜放
  入加糖炒數下，即將其他各絲加入
  兜勻。灒酒加上湯續煮 1 分鐘。試
  合味以生粉水和成饡汁。放入葱再
  兜數下，即可上碟。

Ingredients:

4 oz (112 g) preserved vegetables
2 cups salted water
4 oz (112 g) carrots
4 oz (112 g) bamboo shoots or
　　cabbage
2 cups boiling water
6 cooked Chinese mushrooms
2 spring onions
1 garlic clove
3 tbsp corn oil

Seasoning-
2 tsp sugar
1 tsp wine
¼ cup stock
2 tsp light soy
a pinch of pepper

Gravy mix-
½ tsp cornflour
½ tbsp water
¼ tsp dark soy
1 tsp sesame oil

Method:

* Soak the preserved vegetables in
  the salted water for 2 hours. Rinse
  under a running tap and drain.
  Cut into 1" (2.5 cm) sections then
  parch in a hot wok over low heat
  till dried.
* Peel and shred the carrots and
  bamboo shoots into similar size to
  the preserved vegetables then
  blanch in the boiling water.
  Refresh and drain.
* Shred the mushrooms. Wash and
  section the spring onions. Slice the
  garlic.
* Heat the wok with the oil to sauté
  the garlic till aromatic. Add the
  preserved vegetables and sugar to
  stir well. Pour in the remaining
  ingredients to mix thoroughly.
  Sizzle the wine and add the stock
  to cook for a minute. Adjust the
  flavour and thicken the sauce with
  the gravy mix. Scatter the spring
  onions to toss thoroughly then
  dish.

素 會 鮑 魚
Sliced Gluten in Oyster Sauce

材料：

麵筋 1 磅（½公斤）	味精½茶匙
鮑魚菇 8 安（224克）	菜油 4 湯匙
沸水 3 杯	羗 2 片
生菜 8 安（224克）	葱頭 1 粒
鹽 1 湯匙	蒜頭 1 粒
糖 1 湯匙	炸油½鑊

麵筋醃料—生抽 1½茶匙	水 2 湯匙
糖½茶匙	胡椒粉少許
酒½茶匙	蔴油½茶匙
味精¼茶匙	

調味——鹽½茶匙	生抽½茶匙
酒 1 茶匙	糖 1 茶匙
上湯½杯	胡椒粉少許
蠔油 1 湯匙	

饋料——生粉 1 茶匙	
水 1 湯匙	
蔴油½茶匙	

製法：

* 麵筋洗淨切片，放入醃料中醃半小時。
* 鮑魚菇片開，放於沸水中飛水。過冷河隔乾水份。沸水留起候用。
* 生菜放於以上沸水中加鹽，糖，味精及 2 湯匙油略拖後撈起，隔乾水份排放碟中。羗片，葱，蒜頭一同拍扁。
* 炸油煮沸，放入麵筋片炸 2 分鐘至金黃色。撈起隔去餘油，冲洗乾淨。
* 再燒紅鑊加入餘油 2 湯匙煮沸，洒鹽爆香羗，葱，蒜頭棄去。將鮑魚菇倒入略炒數秒鐘。即加麵筋片潰酒兜勻。再加上湯及調味料試至合味，以生粉水埋饋，盛在生菜上即成。

Ingredients:

1 lb (½ kg) cooked gluten balls
8 oz (¼ kg) abalone mushrooms
3 cups boiling water
8 oz (¼ kg) lettuce
1 tbsp salt
1 tbsp sugar
½ tsp M.S.G.
4 tbsp corn oil
2 slices ginger
1 shallot
1 garlic clove
½ wok oil for deep frying

Gluten Marinade-	Seasoning-
1½ tsp light soy	½ tsp salt
½ tsp sugar	1 tsp wine
½ tsp wine	½ cup stock
¼ tsp M.S.G.	1 tbsp oyster sauce
2 tbsp water	½ tsp light soy
a pinch of pepper	1 tsp sugar
½ tsp sesame oil	a dash of pepper

Gravy Mix-
1 tsp cornflour
1 tbsp water
½ tsp sesame oil

Method:

* Wash and slice the gluten balls into pieces. Soak in the marinade for half an hour.
* Cut the abalone mushrooms into halves and blanch in the boiling water. Refresh and drain. Keep the boiling water for later use.
* Wash and blanch the lettuce in the same boiling water with the salt, sugar, M.S.G. and 2 tbsp of the oil. Drain and dish on to a plate. Mash the ginger, shallot and garlic.
* Bring the ½ wok of oil to the boil. Deep fry the gluten slices for 2 minutes till light brown. Remove, refresh and drain.
* Reheat the work to bring the remaining 2 tbsp oil to the boil. Sprinkle in the salt and sauté the ginger, shallot and garlic till aromatic. Discard. Put in the abalone mushrooms to stir fry for a few seconds. Add the gluten slices and sizzle the wine. Pour in the stock and season to taste. Thicken the sauce with the gravy mix. Scoop on to the lettuce and serve hot.

軟 滑 豆 腐
Soft Beancurd

材料：

黃豆24安（784克）
水25杯
石膏粉 5 茶匙
另水½杯

特別用具：

篩 1 個
紗布袋 1 個
毛巾 1 條
12吋（30公分）丁方不銹鋼板 2 塊
10吋（25公分）丁方鋼方格 1 個
20吋（50公分）丁方紗布 1 塊
9⅜吋（24公分）丁方鋼蓋 1 件

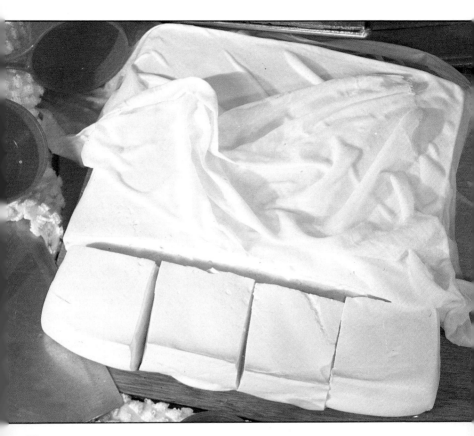

製法：

* 黃豆以清水蓋面浸 8 至12小時，清洗乾淨隔去水份。
* 將黃豆放於搞拌機內約一半滿，倒入水 1 ½ 杯。用中等速度打約30秒至幼，將餘下豆全部搞爛。用密篩隔去豆渣，再放入紗布袋內用力壓豆渣使能搾出更多豆漿。
* 隔妥之豆漿與水混和至共成25杯，置深煲內以文火煮沸。
* 石膏粉溶解於 ½ 杯水中，將石膏粉水與豆漿一同冲入大盆內，用毛巾蓋密放置一旁 5 分鐘使凝結成豆腐花。
* 將一塊12吋丁方之鋼板平放在桌上，架上10吋丁方之四方格，鋪上紗布，將半凝結之豆腐盛在方格中。紗布四邊覆入蓋面，上放不銹鋼蓋再用 6 磅（ 3 公斤）重之重物壓去水份。約需 1 小時。
* 移去重物將紗布揭開，用另一塊12吋丁方鋼板蓋着，將豆腐倒置在鋼板上，除去方格及紗布將豆腐分切成 3 吋× 3 吋（ 7.5 公分× 7.5 公分）正方大件，然後浸在一盆凍水中，存放在雪柜內隨時取用，但須緊記每天更換清水以防變酸。

Ingredients:

24 oz (784 g) soya beans
25 cups water
5 tsp plaster of Paris
an extra ½ cup water

Special Equipments:

1 sieve
1 muslin bag
1 towel
2 stainless steel sheets measuring 12" × 12" (30 cm × 30 cm)
a 10" × 10" (25 cm × 25 cm) bottomless mould
a 20" × 20" (50cm × 50cm) muslin cloth
a stainless steel lid measuring 9¾" × 9¾" (24 cm × 24 cm)

Method:

* *Pour in enough water to cover the soya beans and soak for 8 to 12 hours. Wash and drain.*
* *Half fill a blender with the beans then pour in 1½ cups of water. Blend on maximum speed for 30 seconds. Repeat to finish grinding all the beans. Remove the sediment with a sieve then put in a muslin bag to press out as much water as you could from the sediment. This liquid is the soya bean milk.*
* *Add the water into the soya bean milk to make up to a total amount of 25 cups. Pour it into a deep saucepan and bring to the boil over low heat.*
* *Dissolve the plaster of Paris in the extra ½ cup of water. Pour the plaster solution and the milk simultaneously into a big container. Cover with the towel and leave to set for 5 minutes to form beancurd jelly.*
* *Place the 12 sq. in. stainless steel sheet on the table top. Put the 10 sq. in. mould on top of the sheet and line it with the muslin cloth. Transfer the half-set jelly into the cloth-lined mould and fold up the cloth to enclose the beancurd jelly. Add the stainless steel lid on top of the covered jelly and put a 6 lb (3 kg) weight on it in order to press out all the excess liquid. Leave aside for an hour.*
* *Remove the weight and the lid, uncover the beancurd and place the other 12 sq. in. stainless steel sheet on top. Turn the whole mould upside down and remove the square mould and muslin cloth. The set beancurd is now ready to be cut into 3" × 3" (7.5 cm × 7.5 cm) square blocks. Keep in a bowl of cold water inside the refrigerator for further usage. It is important to change the water daily in order to prevent the beancurd from turning sour.*

絲瓜豆乾

Spiced Beancurd with Courgettes

材料：

絲瓜10安（280克）
凍水3杯
豆腐乾3件
馬蹄6粒
木耳¼安（7克）
沸水1½杯
紅蘿蔔12片
熟冬菇4隻
羌2片
葱頭1粒
菜油2湯匙

調味—鹽¼茶匙
　　　酒1茶匙
　　　上湯¼杯
　　　生抽1茶匙
　　　糖½茶匙
　　　胡椒粉少許

饋料—生粉½茶匙
　　　水1湯匙
　　　老抽¼茶匙
　　　蔴油1茶匙

製法：

* 絲瓜去皮切三角形，以凍水2杯浸住候用。
* 豆腐乾洗淨片開。馬蹄去皮洗淨亦片開。
* 木耳以其餘1杯凍水浸透。剪去蒂後與紅蘿蔔片一同放沸水中飛水片刻。隔乾水份將木耳切件候用。
* 熟冬菇片開。羌切絲。葱頭切片。
* 燒紅鑊加油煮沸，洒下鹽爆香羌，葱片。隨即傾入木耳，絲瓜及馬蹄略炒數下。即下其他配料兜勻。讚酒加上湯及調味料，生粉水加其他饋料和勻慢慢流入拌勻，再滴入蔴油拋勻上碟。

Ingredients:

10 oz (280 g) courgettes
3 cups cold water
3 pieces spiced beancurd
6 water chestnuts
¼ oz (7 g) black fungus
1½ cups boiling water
12 slices carrot
4 cooked Chinese mushrooms
2 slices ginger
1 shallot
2 tbsp corn oil

Seasoning-
¼ tsp salt
1 tsp wine
¼ cup stock
1 tsp light soy
½ tsp sugar
a pinch of pepper

Gravy mix-
½ tsp cornflour
1 tbsp water
¼ tsp dark soy
1 tsp sesame oil

Method:

* *Peel and wedge the courgettes. Soak in 2 cups of the cold water for later use.*
* *Clean and slice the spiced beancurd. Peel, wash and slice the water chestnuts.*
* *Soak the fungus in the remaining cup of cold water until softened. Trim and blanch in the boiling water together with the sliced carrots. Refresh and cut the fungus into pieces.*
* *Slice the mushrooms. Shred the ginger and slice the shallot.*
* *Heat the wok with the oil and sprinkle in the salt. Stir in the ginger, shallot, fungus, courgettes and water chestnuts to fry well. Add the remaining ingredients then sizzle the wine. Pour in the stock and seasoning. Stream in the gravy mix to thicken the sauce. Drop in the sesame oil to toss evenly and dish.*

五 香 素 卷
Spicy Beancurd Rolls

材料：

佛手瓜或青瓜 6 安（168克）　　沸水 1 杯　　　　調味—香鹽 $\frac{1}{2}$ 茶匙

紅蘿蔔 3 安（84克）　　　　　薑 1 片　　　　　　　　　酒 1 茶匙

熟冬菇 2 安（56克）　　　　　菜油 2 湯匙　　　　　　上湯 $\frac{1}{4}$ 杯

木耳 $\frac{1}{4}$ 安（ 7 克）　　　　　腐皮 3 張　　　　　　　生抽 $\frac{1}{2}$ 茶匙

凍水 2 杯　　　　　　　　　　另菜油 $\frac{1}{2}$ 杯　　　　　　糖 1 茶匙

　　　　　　　　　　　　　　　　　　　　　　　　　　胡椒粉少許

饋料—生粉½茶匙
　　　水½湯匙
　　　蔴油½茶匙

汁料—糖2湯匙　　　醋1茶匙
　　　生抽2湯匙　　辣油1茶匙
　　　上湯2湯匙　　五香粉½茶匙
　　　蔴醬1茶匙　　芫茜及辣椒件各少許
　　　蔴油1茶匙

製法：

* 佛手瓜及紅蘿蔔去皮與冬菇同切絲
　。木耳放凍水中浸透修妥洗淨。再
　放沸水中飛水½分鐘，撈起冲水切
　絲。羌亦切絲。

* 燒紅鑊加油2湯匙煮沸，洒鹽傾入
　木耳爆炒10秒鐘。隨即加入羌絲、
　佛手瓜及紅蘿蔔絲拌炒數下。再加
　冬菇絲兜勻。潷酒加上湯及調妥味
　後以生粉水埋饋。盛在碟中攤凍，
　分作12份候用。

* 腐皮抹淨修剪妥當，每張剪為四個
　三角形，將一份餡料放在每張三角
　腐皮上，捲起包好。重複此做法直
　至將全部腐皮捲完。

* 將鑊洗淨再燒熱，傾入油½杯煮沸
　。將素卷排在油中半煎炸至兩面金
　黃色。取出放在長碟中，每卷斜剪
　為兩段。

* 汁料放在碗中拌勻後淋在腐皮卷上
　即可上桌。

Ingredients:

6 oz (168 g) choco or cucumber
3 oz (84 g) carrots
2 oz (56 g) cooked Chinese mushrooms
¼ oz (7 g) hard black fungus
2 cups cold water
1 cup boiling water
1 slice ginger
2 tbsp corn oil
3 beancurd sheets
½ cup corn oil for shallow frying

Seasoning-
½ tsp spicy salt　　½ tsp light soy
1 tsp wine　　　　½ tsp sugar
¼ cup stock　　　a pinch of pepper

Gravy Mix-
½ tsp cornflour
½ tbsp water
½ tsp sesame oil

Condiment Mix-
2 tbsp sugar
2 tbsp light soy
2 tbsp stock
1 tsp sesame paste
1 tsp sesame oil
1 tsp vinegar
1 tsp chilli oil
½ tsp 5-spice powder
chopped parsley and chillies

Method:

* Peel and shred the choco, carrots
and mushrooms. Soak the black
fungus in the cold water until soft.
Trim, wash and blanch in the
boiling water for half a minute.
Refresh, drain and shred. Shred
the ginger.

* Heat the wok with the 2 tbsp oil
and sprinkle in the salt to sauté the
black fungus for 10 seconds. Stir
in the shredded ginger, choco and
carrots to fry over moderate heat.
Add the mushrooms to mix well.
Sizzle the wine, pour in the stock
and season to taste. Thicken the
sauce with the garvy mix. Dish and
leave to cool. Divide into 12
portions for later use.

* Wipe and trim the beancurd
sheets. Cut each round sheet into
4 parts. Place 1 portion of filling
on to each part and roll up tightly.
Repeat until 12 rolls are made.

* Clean and reheat the wok with the
½ cup of oil. Arrange the rolls to
shallow fry till both sides are
golden. Remove on to an oval
platter and cut each roll into
halves.

* Stir the condiment mix evenly and
adjust the flavour according to
taste. Pour over the rolls and
serve.

八 珍 腐 球

Stewed Beancurd with Assorted Vegetables

材料：

板豆腐 3 件
鹽 1 茶匙
炸油 5 杯
草菇 5 隻
白果 8 粒
木耳¼安（7 克）
沸水 2 杯
紅蘿蔔 10 片
珍珠筍 3 安（84 克）
青瓜 4 安（112 克）
馬蹄 5 粒
菜油 2 湯匙
蒜頭 1 片
熟冬菇 5 隻

調味—鹽½茶匙　　饐料—生粉 1 茶匙
　　　酒 1 茶匙　　　　　水 1 湯匙
　　　上湯½杯　　　　　老抽½茶匙
　　　蠔油 1 湯匙　　　　蔴油 1 茶匙
　　　糖½茶匙
　　　胡椒粉少許

製法：

*　板豆腐切三角件，以鹽洒勻。燒紅
　鑊倒下炸油煮沸，將板豆腐逐件滑
　入炸至金黃色，撈起隔淨餘油。
*　草菇削淨。白果去売去衣。木耳浸
　透後與白果，紅蘿蔔及珍珠筍一同
　放沸水中飛水，撈起冲凍隔乾水份。
*　青瓜，馬蹄去皮切片。
*　燒紅鑊加油 2 湯匙煮沸，洒下鹽炸
　香蒜片。將菇類及雜菜全部放入炒
　勻。傾下豆腐潷酒加上湯及調味料
　煮片刻。試妥味後以生粉水埋饐，
　老抽及蔴油滴入後即可上碟。

Ingredients:

3 pieces beancurd
1 tsp salt
5 cups oil for deep frying
5 straw mushrooms
8 ginkgo nuts
¼ oz (7 g) black fungus
2 cups boiling water
10 pieces carrot
3 oz (84 g) baby corns
4 oz (112 g) cucumber
5 water chestnuts
2 tbsp corn oil
1 sliced garlic
5 cooked Chinese mushrooms

Seasoning-
½ tsp salt
1 tsp wine
½ cup stock
1 tbsp oyster sauce
½ tsp sugar
a pinch of pepper

Gravy Mix-
1 tsp cornflour
1 tbsp water
½ tsp dark soy
1 tsp sesame oil

Method:

*　Wedge and dust the beancurd
　with the salt. Heat the wok and
　pour in the oil to bring to the boil.
　Slide the beancurd into the hot oil
　and deep fry till golden brown.
　Drain.
*　Trim the straw mushrooms and
　shell the ginkgo nuts. Soak the
　black fungus and blanch in the
　boiling water together with the
　ginkgo nuts, carrots and baby
　corns. Refresh and drain.
*　Peel and slice the cucumber and
　water chestnuts.
*　Heat the wok till very hot, bring
　the oil to the boil and sprinkle in
　the salt. Sauté the garlic till
　aromatic. Pour in the assorted
　mushrooms and vegetables to stir
　well. Add the beancurd then sizzle
　the wine, mix in the stock and
　seasoning and adjust the flavour.
　Thicken the sauce with the gravy
　mix. Drop in the dark soy and
　sesame oil then dish.

冬 菇 麵 筋

Stewed Gluten Rolls with Mushrooms

材料：

熟冬菇 2 安（56克）
金針 2 安（56克）
沸水 3 杯
木耳 ½ 安（14克）
麵筋 12 安（336克）
炸油 4 杯
羌 2 片
葱頭 2 粒
蒜頭 1 粒
菜油 2 湯匙

調味—鹽 ½ 茶匙
　　　酒 1 茶匙
　　　冬菇水 ¾ 杯
　　　生抽 1 茶匙
　　　蠔油 1 湯匙
　　　糖 1 茶匙
　　　胡椒粉少許

饋料—生粉 1 茶匙
　　　水 1 湯匙
　　　蔴油 1 茶匙

製法：

* 熟冬菇每隻分切兩邊候用。
* 金針放入 1 杯沸水中浸至軟，剪去頭尾洗淨。每兩條打 1 個結。
* 木耳放於另 1 杯沸水中浸透，剪去硬蒂洗淨切成小件。放入其餘沸水中飛水，撈起冲隔乾水份。
* 麵筋分切成小件，放沸油中炸至金黃色。盛起隔乾餘油後。置水喉下冲洗乾淨。
* 羌片切絲。葱，蒜頭切片。
* 燒紅鑊加油煮沸，洒鹽爆香羌，葱，蒜。倒入木耳，麵筋及冬菇兜炒 ½ 分鐘。瀢酒加冬菇水，蓋上鑊蓋以文火炆 5 分鐘。揭蓋加入金針及餘下調味料續煮 5 分鐘，以生粉水打饋上碟。

Ingredients:

2 oz (56 g) cooked Chinese mush-
　rooms
2 oz (56 g) dried lily buds
3 cups boiling water
½ oz (14 g) hard black fungus
12 oz (336 g) gluten rolls
4 cups hot oil for deep frying
2 slices ginger
2 shallots
1 garlic clove
2 tbsp corn oil

Seasoning-
½ tsp salt
1 tsp wine
¾ cup mushroom water
1 tsp light soy
1 tbsp oyster sauce
1 tsp sugar
a pinch of pepper

Gravy Mix-
1 tsp cornflour
1 tbsp water
1 tsp sesame oil

Method:

* *Halve the cooked mushrooms.*
* *Soak the lily buds with 1 cup of the boiling water until soft. Trim, clean and tie every two pieces into one knot.*
* *Soak the black fungus in another cup of the boiling water. Trim, clean and section the fungus. Blanch in the remaining cup of boiling water. Refresh and drain.*
* *Cut the gluten rolls into small pieces. Deep fry them in the hot oil till golden brown. Drain and rinse under a running tap.*
* *Shred the ginger. Slice the shallots and garlic.*
* *Heat the wok with the oil and sprinkle in the salt. Sauté the ginger, shallots and garlic till aromatic. Put in the fungus, gluten, and mushrooms to stir fry for half a minute. Sizzle the wine and pour in the mushroom water. Cover to simmer for 5 minutes over low heat. Remove the lid and add the lily buds and the rest of the seasoning. Continue to cook for a further 5 minutes. Thicken the sauce with the gravy mix and dish.*

红 烧 素 丸

Stewed Potato Balls

材料：

熟薯仔12安（336克）	蒜頭1粒
馬蹄10安（280克）	生菜數塊
紅蘿蔔1安（28克）	麵粉1安（28克）
豆腐乾2件	生粉½杯塗面用
榨菜1安（28克）	炸油½杯
熟冬菇1安（28克）	菜油3湯匙
羌2片	

調味——鹽½茶匙
　　　老抽1湯匙
　　　糖1茶匙
　　　胡椒粉少許
　　　蔴油1茶匙

汁——酒1茶匙
　　　上湯½杯
　　　生抽1茶匙
　　　糖½茶匙

製法：

* 熟薯仔去皮放大盆中搓爛成伴。馬蹄去皮磨爛。紅蘿蔔，豆腐乾，榨菜，冬菇及羌皆切幼粒。

* 蒜頭切片。生菜洗淨隔乾排放在碟上置一旁候用。用小碗將調味料撈勻。

* 將全部伴及切幼之材料放入盆中，加入撈勻之調味料及麵粉撈勻成薯泥試合味。

* 將薯泥以手做成小丸放在乾生粉中打滾。用煮沸炸油炸至金黃色撈起。

* 另鑊燒紅加油2湯匙煮沸爆香蒜片。潠酒加上湯及調味料，將薯丸傾回鑊中炆5分鐘至汁濃縮成饍。洒入餘下1湯匙油拌勻，盛在已墊生菜之碟中上桌。

Ingredients:

12 oz (336 g) cooked potatoes
10 oz (280 g) water chestnuts
1 oz (28 g) carrots
2 pieces spiced beancurd
1 oz (28 g) preserved mustard
*1 oz (28 g) cooked Chinese
  mushrooms*
2 slices ginger
1 garlic clove
a few lettuce leaves
1 oz (28 g) flour
½ cup cornflour for coating
½ wok hot oil for deep frying
3 tbsp corn oil

Seasoning-
½ tsp salt
1 tbsp dark soy
1 tsp sugar
a pinch of pepper
1 tsp sesame oil

Sauce-
1 tsp wine
½ cup stock
1 tsp light soy
½ tsp sugar

Method:

* *Peel and mash the cooked potatoes. Peel and grate the water chestnuts. Dice the carrots, beancurd, mustard, mushrooms and the ginger finely.*
* *Slice the garlic. Wash and drain the lettuce. Arrange into a serving bowl and leave aside for later use. Mix the seasoning in a small bowl.*
* *Place all the ingredients in a mixing bowl then add the mixed seasoning and the flour to stir well.*
* *Shape the mixture into small balls and coat with the cornflour. Bring the oil to boil in a wok and deep fry the potato balls until golden brown. Drain.*
* *Heat the wok and add 2 tbsp oil to sauté the garlic. Sprinkle the wine, add the stock and seasoning. Put in the potato balls to simmer for 5 minutes until a little sauce is left. Lastly drop in the remaining tbsp of oil to mix well and dish on to the bed of raw lettuce.*

豉 汁 茄 夾

Stuffed Eggplant in Black Bean Sauce

材料：

馬蹄10安（280克）	茄子12安（336克）
榨菜1安（28克）	生粉3湯匙
熟冬菇3隻	菜油4湯匙
豆腐乾2件	蒜頭2粒
葱粒2湯匙	

調味——鹽 $\frac{1}{4}$ 茶匙
　　　　糖 $\frac{1}{2}$ 茶匙
　　　　胡椒粉少許
　　　　生粉1茶匙

豉汁饋——酒1茶匙
　　　　上湯 $\frac{1}{2}$ 杯
　　　　豆豉醬2湯匙
　　　　生抽 $\frac{1}{2}$ 茶匙
　　　　糖 $\frac{1}{2}$ 茶匙
　　　　生粉1茶匙
　　　　水1湯匙
　　　　蔴油 $\frac{1}{2}$ 茶匙

製法：

* 馬蹄去皮洗淨磨爛成茸。
* 榨菜，冬菇及豆腐乾皆切幼粒。與馬蹄茸一同放在大盆中。加葱粒及調味料以手撻至起膠。置雪柜內雪 $\frac{1}{2}$ 小時。
* 茄子洗淨斜切成 $\frac{1}{2}$ 吋（1.25公分）厚片，中割一條裂縫使成袋形。在袋中輕撲生粉，隨將馬蹄茸以刀釀入。
* ·燒紅鑊加油3湯匙煮沸，爆香蒜頭後置一旁候用。將茄夾逐件滑入油中煎至兩面金黃色取出。
* 鑊中再放餘油1湯匙煮沸。將蒜頭重放入內爆香棄去。潷酒加上湯，豆豉醬，生抽及糖。將茄夾重放鑊中文火煮4分鐘，以生粉加水和成饋。再滴入蔴油拌勻即可上碟。

Ingredients:

10 oz (280 g) water chestnuts
1 oz (28 g) preserved mustard
3 cooked Chinese mushrooms
2 pieces spiced beancurd
2 tbsp chopped spring onions
12 oz (336 g) eggplant
3 tbsp cornflour
4 tbsp corn oil
2 garlic cloves

Seasoning-
¼ tsp salt
½ tsp sugar
a pinch of pepper
1 tsp cornflour

Black Bean Sauce-
1 tsp wine
½ cup stock
2 tbsp fermented black bean paste
½ tsp light soy
½ tsp sugar
1 tsp cornflour
1 tbsp water
½ tsp sesame oil

Method:

* *Peel, wash and grate the water chestnuts.*
* *Dice the preserved mustard, mushrooms and beancurd finely. Put into a mixing bowl together with the water chestnuts and spring onions. Add the seasoning to mix well and pound until firm. Keep in the refrigerator for 30 minutes.*
* *Cut the eggplant into ½" (1.25 cm) thick pieces with a slit in the centre of each. Dust the slit with the cornflour then fill with the mashed water chestnut filling.*
* *Heat the wok till hot and bring 3 tbsp of the oil to the boil. Sauté the garlic then remove and retain for later use. Slide the stuffed eggplant into the wok to shallow fry till both sides are golden brown. Remove.*
* *Bring the other tbsp of oil to the boil in the wok. Sauté the garlic again and discard. Sizzle the wine, pour in the stock and add the bean paste, light soy, sugar and stuffed eggplants to simmer for 4 minutes. Mix the cornflour with the water, then slowly stream into the sauce to thicken. Drop in the sesame oil to mix thoroughly and dish.*

佛 法 蒲 團

Stuffed Gluten Balls

材料：

生筋球20隻	菜油 5 湯匙
沸水 4 杯	紅蘿蔔茸 2 湯匙
草菰 6 隻	栗子茸 1 杯
白果 6 粒	榨菜茸 2 湯匙
馬蹄10粒	青豆 2 湯匙
熟冬菇 4 隻	生粉 $\frac{1}{2}$ 杯

調味—酒 $\frac{1}{2}$ 茶匙　　　　醃料—生粉 $\frac{1}{2}$ 茶匙
　　　上湯 3 湯匙　　　　　　水 $\frac{1}{2}$ 湯匙
　　　鹽 $\frac{1}{4}$ 茶匙　　　　　　蔴油 $\frac{1}{2}$ 茶匙
　　　糖 1 茶匙
　　　蠔油 1 茶匙
　　　胡椒粉少許

製法：

* 生筋球放於 3 杯沸水中飛水約30秒鐘以去油味。取出放水喉下沖洗後揸乾水份。
* 草菰洗淨削去蒂。白果去壳去衣。馬蹄去皮洗淨。將草菰及白果放入其餘 1 杯沸水中飛水。撈起沖淨隔乾水份。將全部用料及冬菇皆切幼粒候用。
* 燒紅鑊加油 2 湯匙煮沸，放入各粒，紅蘿蔔茸，栗子茸及其他材料爆炒均勻。潷酒加上湯及調味料拌勻試妥味。即以生粉水埋饋，盛在碟上攤凍。並將餡料分爲20份候用。
* 生筋每隻在中央剪開，內塗少許生粉。放入餡料 1 份，滾上一層乾生粉。
* 另鑊燒紅加入餘油 3 湯匙煮沸，將釀妥之生筋球滑入半煎炸至兩面金黃色。盛在碟上熱食。喜愛汁液者，可以生粉水加老抽打饋淋在上面。

Ingredients:

20 puffed gluten balls
4 cups boiling water
6 straw mushrooms
6 ginkgo nuts
10 water chestnuts
4 cooked Chinese mushrooms
5 tbsp corn oil
2 tbsp grated carrots
1 cup chestnut purée
2 tbsp minced preserved mustard
2 tbsp sweet peas
½ cup cornflour

Seasoning-
½ tsp wine
3 tbsp stock
¼ tsp salt
1 tsp sugar
1 tsp oyster sauce
a pinch of pepper

Gravy Mix-
½ tsp cornflour
½ tbsp water
½ tsp sesame oil

Method:

* Blanch the gluten balls in 3 cups of the boiling water to remove the stale odour. Rinse under running cold water and drain.
* Trim and wash the straw mushrooms. Shell and peel the ginkgo nuts. Peel and wash the water chestnuts. Blanch the straw mushrooms and ginkgo nuts in the remaining boiling water then refresh and drain. Dice all these ingredients and the Chinese mushrooms.
* Heat the wok and bring 2 tbsp of the oil to boil. Sauté the diced vegetables, carrots, chestnut purée and all the other ingredients thoroughly. Sizzle the wine and add the stock and seasoning. Season to taste. Thicken the sauce with the gravy mix. Dish and leave aside to cool. Divide into 20 portions.
* Slit each of the gluten ball in the centre. Dust with the cornflour and put in a portion of the filling. Coat with the cornflour again.
* Bring the remaining 3 tbsp of oil to the boil in the wok. Arrange the stuffed gluten balls to shallow fry till both sides are golden. Serve hot. A gravy can be produced in the usual way and mask over the gluten balls if so desired.

素 釀 冬 菇
Stuffed Mushrooms with Potatoes

材料：

冬菇24隻 醃料—鹽 $\frac{1}{8}$ 茶匙
豆腐乾 1 件 糖 $\frac{1}{2}$ 茶匙
紅蘿蔔 1 安（28克） 菜油 1 湯匙
馬蹄 3 安（84克）
薯仔12安（336克） 調味—鹽 $\frac{1}{2}$ 茶匙
葱頭 1 粒 糖 $\frac{1}{2}$ 茶匙
蒜頭 1 粒 胡椒粉少許
生粉 $\frac{1}{4}$ 杯 生粉 1 至 2 湯匙
青豆24粒 蛋白 $\frac{1}{2}$ 隻
菜油 2 湯匙

饀料—上湯 $\frac{1}{2}$ 杯
   蠔油 1 茶匙
   生抽 1 茶匙
   糖 1 茶匙
   生粉 1 茶匙
   蔴油 1 茶匙

製法：

* 冬菇洗淨浸透剪去蒂，以醃料略醃
  後蒸12分鐘。置一旁候用。
* 豆腐乾及紅蘿蔔洗淨剁成茸，放入
  大盆中。
* 馬蹄及薯仔去皮磨爛，揸乾水份加
  入盆中與紅蘿蔔撈勻。
* 調味料混和加入混合物中撻勻。葱
  ，蒜頭拍扁。
* 冬菇內洒少許生粉。將每隻冬菇放
  入饀料 1 湯匙，另置青豆在上面點
  綴。將冬菇排放在碟上置蒸籠內蒸
  10分鐘取出。
* 燒紅鑊加油煮沸爆香葱，蒜頭棄去
  。加入拌勻之饀料再煮沸。隨即把
  饀汁淋在已釀妥之冬菇上，即可上
  桌。

Ingredients:

24 Chinese dried mushrooms
1 piece spiced beancurd
1 oz (28 g) carrots
3 oz (84 g) water chestnuts
12 oz (336 g) potatoes
1 shallot
1 garlic clove
¼ cup cornflour
24 sweet peas
2 tbsp corn oil

Mushrooms Marinade-
⅛ tsp salt
½ tsp sugar
1 tbsp corn oil

Seasoning-
½ tsp salt
½ tsp sugar
a pinch of pepper
1 to 2 tbsp cornflour
½ egg white

Gravy Mix-
½ cup stock
1 tsp oyster sauce
1 tsp light soy
1 tsp sugar
1 tsp cornflour
1 tsp sesame oil

Method:

* Wash, trim, soak and mix the
  mushrooms with the marinade.
  Steam for 12 minutes. Leave aside
  for later use.
* Wash and mince the spicy beancurd and carrots then place in a
  mixing bowl.
* Peel and grate the water chestnuts
  and potatoes. Squeeze out the
  water and add to the carrot
  mixture.
* Put the seasoning in a small bowl
  to mix well then stir into the above
  mixture and bind well. Mash the
  shallot and garlic.
* Dust the cornflour on the inside of
  the mushrooms and stuff 1 tbsp of
  filling on to each. Garnish with a
  sweet pea on top. Place the stuffed
  mushrooms on a plate and steam
  for 10 minutes. Remove.
* Heat the wok with the oil to sauté
  the shallot and garlic till aromatic.
  Discard. Pour in the gravy mix
  and bring to the boil. Mask over
  the stuffed mushrooms and dish.

蜜味素腎

Sweet and Hot Gluten

材料：

麵筋 1 磅（½公斤）
沸水 3 杯
炸油½鑊
辣椒乾 5 隻
羌 2 片
葱頭 2 粒
菜油 2 湯匙
糖膠¼杯

調味—酒 1 茶匙
　　　上湯½杯
　　　老抽 2 湯匙
　　　糖 2 湯匙
　　　味精¼茶匙
　　　胡椒粉少許
　　　蔴油 1 茶匙

製法：

* 麵筋放於沸水中飛水，洗淨切粒。燒紅鑊煮沸炸油，放入麵筋炸至金黃色，撈起置水喉下沖洗後隔乾水份。

* 辣椒乾去籽洗淨切絲。羌，葱頭去皮拍扁。

* 另鑊燒紅加油煮沸，爆香羌，葱頭後棄去。

* 紅椒絲放入爆香，再加麵筋粒炒透。灒酒加上湯及調味料續煮至水份將乾時，即可加入糖膠兜勻，盛在淺焗盤上放入預熱 300 度（煤氣 2 度）之焗爐內焗乾或置太陽下晒乾。

Ingredients:

1 lb (½ kg) cooked gluten balls
3 cups boiling water
½ wok hot oil for deep frying
5 dried chillies
2 slices ginger
2 shallots
2 tbsp corn oil
¼ cup corn syrup

Seasoning-
1 tsp wine
½ cup stock
2 tbsp dark soy
2 tbsp sugar
¼ tsp M.S.G.
a pinch of pepper
1 tsp sesame oil

Method:

* *Blanch the gluten balls in the boiling water, wash and dice. Bring the oil to boil in the wok and deep fry the gluten balls in the hot oil till golden brown. Refresh under the running tap and drain.*

* *Deseed, wash and shred the dried chillies. Peel and mash the ginger and shallots.*

* *Heat the wok with the oil to sauté the ginger and shallots then discard.*

* *Stir in the shredded chillies to sauté till pungent. Mix in the diced gluten to fry thoroughly. Sizzle the wine, pour in the stock and seasoning. Simmer until the stock nearly dries up. Drop in the corn syrup to toss well. Remove and dry in a preheated 300°F (Gas Mark 2) oven or under the sun.*

甜 酸 豆 腐

Sweet and Sour Beancurd

材料：

馬蹄½磅（224克）
冬菇粒 1 湯匙
紅蘿蔔粒 1 茶匙
蛋白 2 隻
胡椒粉少許
麵粉½茶匙
豆腐 12 安（336 克）
葱 2 條切粒
生粉½杯
炸油 3 杯
另菜油 1 湯匙

調味——鹽½茶匙
　　　糖½茶匙
　　　胡椒粉少許
　　　蔴油 1 茶匙
　　　生粉 1 至 2 湯匙

甜酸饡—酒 1 茶匙
　　　甜酸醋½杯
　　　生粉 1 茶匙
　　　水 1 湯匙
　　　五柳料 1 湯匙

製法：

* 馬蹄去皮洗淨磨爛。加入冬菇粒，
  紅蘿蔔粒、1 隻蛋白，胡椒粉及麵
  粉搞成糊，再撻至硬身。
* 豆腐搞爛成粒，與另 1 隻蛋白加入
  馬蹄粒中再加葱粒及調味料和勻。
  倒在一個塗油方盤內以手撳平。放
  在蒸籠內蒸 8 分鐘，取出攤凍切成
  長方片。放在乾生粉上滾上一層粉。
* 燒紅鑊將炸油傾下煮沸。將豆腐片
  滑入炸至金黃色，撈起隔去餘油。
* 再燒紅鑊加油 1 湯匙煮沸。潷酒倒
  入甜酸醋。待重沸時即將生粉水流
  下和成濃饡，淋在豆腐上立刻上碟
  ，加五柳料在上即成。

Ingredients:

½ lb (224 g) water chestnuts
1 tbsp diced Chinese mushrooms
1 tsp minced carrots
2 egg white
a pinch of pepper
½ tsp plain flour
12 oz (336 g) beancurd
2 spring onions (chopped)
½ cup cornflour
3 cups oil for deep frying
1 tbsp corn oil

Seasoning-
½ tsp salt
½ tsp sugar
a pinch of pepper
1 tsp sesame oil
1 to 2 tbsp cornflour

Sweet Sour Sauce-
1 tsp wine
½ cup sweet sour sauce
1 tsp cornflour
1 tbsp water
1 tbsp pickled gherkin

Method:

* Peel, wash and grate the water
  chestnuts. Add the mushrooms,
  carrots, an egg white, the pepper,
  and the flour to bind into a paste
  then pound until firm.
* Mash the beancurd into a purée.
  Add the mashed beancurd, the
  other egg white, the chopped
  spring onions and seasoning to the
  water chestnut mixture and bind
  well. Pour in to a greased sand-
  wich tin to steam for 8 minutes.
  Remove and leave aside to cool.
  Cut into pieces then coat with the
  cornflour.
* Heat the wok until hot. Pour in
  the oil to bring to the boil. Slide in
  the beancurd to deep fry until
  golden. Drain and dish.
* Reheat the wok with the 1 tbsp of
  oil. Sizzle the wine and drop in the
  sweet sour sauce to bring to the
  boil. Mix the cornflour with the
  water then trickle into the sauce to
  thicken. Pour on to the beancurd
  and sprinkle the pickled gherkin.
  Serve hot.

素 咕 嚕 肉
Sweet and Sour Walnuts

材料：

合桃肉 5 安（140克）
沸水 3 杯
炸油 4 杯
洋葱 3 安（84克）
菠蘿 2 片

紅椒 1 隻
青椒 1 隻
蒜頭 1 粒
葱 1 棵
菜油 2 湯匙

脆漿—麵粉 1 杯
　　　生粉 1 湯匙
　　　發粉 2 茶匙
　　　水 ½ 杯
　　　菜油 1 湯匙

調味—鹽 ¼ 茶匙
　　　酒 1 茶匙
　　　甜酸醋 ½ 杯
　　　生抽 1 茶匙
　　　糖 1 茶匙
　　　胡椒粉少許

饙料—生粉 1 茶匙
　　　水 1 湯匙
　　　蔴油 1 茶匙

製法：

* 合桃肉放沸水中浸30分鐘，撈起置已預熱250度（煤氣½度）之焗爐中烘25分鐘至鬆脆。
* 麵粉，生粉及發粉一同篩在碗中，加水和成濃漿。放置一旁發½小時，將油拌入再發15分鐘。
* 把合桃逐件放入漿中滾滿脆漿後，即放熱油中炸至金黃色。撈起隔除油。
* 洋蔥去皮洗淨切件。菠蘿切細件。青紅椒去籽亦切件。蒜頭切片。蔥切度。
* 燒紅鑊加油,煮沸,洒鹽爆香蒜片。倒入切件洋蔥及青紅椒猛火炒½分鐘。讚酒加甜酸醋及調味煮沸試妥味後，以生粉水埋饙，再將菠蘿及炸合桃拌入兜勻。洒蔥度上碟熱食。

Ingredients:

5 oz (140 g) shelled walnuts
3 cups boiling water
4 cups hot oil for deep frying
3 oz (84 g) onions
2 tinned pineapple rings
1 chilli
1 capsicum
1 garlic clove
1 spring onion
2 tbsp corn oil

Batter-
1 cup plain flour
1 tbsp cornflour
2 tsp baking powder
½ cup water
1 tbsp corn oil

Seasoning-
¼ tsp salt
1 tsp wine
½ cup sweet sour sauce
1 tsp light soy
1 tsp sugar
a pinch of pepper

Gravy Mix-
1 tsp cornflour
1 tbsp water
1 tsp sesame oil

Method:

* *Soak the walnuts in the boiling water for 30 minutes. Drain and toast in a preheated 250°F (Gas Mark ½) oven for 25 minutes or till crisp.*
* *Sift the plain flour, cornflour and baking powder into a mixing bowl. Add the water to bind into a smooth batter and leave aside for half an hour. Blend in the oil and leave for another 15 minutes.*
* *Dip the toasted walnuts in the batter and deep fry in the hot oil till golden then drain.*
* *Peel, wash and cut the onions. Cut the pineapple into smaller pieces. Deseed and cut the chilli and capsicum. Slice the garlic and section the spring onion.*
* *Heat the wok with the oil and sprinkle in the salt. Sauté the garlic till fragrant. Put in the onion, chilli and capsicum to stir fry for half a minute. Sizzle the wine, add the sweet sour sauce and season to taste. Thicken the sauce with the gravy mix. Stir in the pineapple and walnuts to toss well. Scatter the spring onion on top and dish. Serve hot.*

粟米豆腐羹
Sweet Corn and Beancurd Chowder

材料：

草菰12隻
沸水 2 杯
熟冬菇 6 隻
豆腐10安（280克）
紅蘿蔔 2 安（56克）
青豆 2 安（56克）
番茄 1 個
粟米 ½ 罐
菜油 1 湯匙
上湯 6 杯

調味—酒 1 茶匙
　　　鹽 2 茶匙
　　　糖 1 茶匙

饋料—生粉 3 湯匙
　　　水 2 湯匙
　　　胡椒粉少許
　　　蔴油 1 茶匙

製法：

* 草菰洗淨修剪妥當，以沸水煮30秒鐘飛水，轉置水喉下沖凍，隔乾水份切粒，沸水留爲別用。
* 熟冬菇，豆腐及紅蘿蔔亦切粒與青豆一同放入以上沸水中飛水候用。番茄切粒。
* 粟米從罐中取出一半放於大碗中，其餘留作別用。
* 燒紅鑊加油煮沸，潷酒加上湯待重沸時，即可拌入紅蘿蔔及冬菇煮 5 分鐘。再加其餘材料及調味料續煮 3 分鐘。以生粉加水和勻搞入湯內至濃度適中時，即可停火。傾入湯碗內加胡椒粉及蔴油上桌。

Ingredients:

12 straw mushrooms
2 cups boiling water
6 cooked Chinese mushrooms
10 oz (280 g) beancurd
2 oz (56 g) carrots
2 oz (56 g) sweet peas
1 tomato
½ tin sweet corn
1 tbsp corn oil
6 cups stock

Seasoning-
1 tsp wine
2 tsp salt
1 tsp sugar

Gravy Mix-
3 tbsp cornflour
2 tbsp water
a pinch of pepper
1 tsp sesame oil

Method:

* *Trim, wash and blanch the straw mushrooms in the boiling water. Drain and retain the water for later use. Refresh and dice the straw mushrooms.*
* *Dice the Chinese mushrooms, beancurd and carrots then blanch in the same boiling water together with the sweet peas. Dice the tomato.*
* *Remove the sweet corn from the tin and put half of it in a bowl. Keep the rest for other usage.*
* *Heat the wok with the oil, sizzle the wine and pour in the stock to bring to the boil. Stir in the carrots and mushrooms to simmer for 5 minutes. Add the remaining ingredients and seasoning to simmer for another 3 minutes. Mix the cornflour and water together then blend into the soup and thicken. Pour into a serving bowl and add the pepper and sesame oil to serve hot.*

白 汁 雙 蔬

Vegetables in White Sauce

材料：

椰菜花10安（280克）
西蘭花10安（280克）
鹽水 4 杯
羌 2 片
葱頭 1 粒
蒜頭 1 粒
凍水 4 杯
鹽 1 湯匙
糖 1 湯匙
味精 ½ 茶匙
菜油 4 湯匙

調味—鹽 ¼ 茶匙
　　　酒 2 茶匙
　　　糖 1 茶匙
　　　上湯 ½ 杯
　　　淡奶 ½ 杯
　　　胡椒粉少許

饂料—生粉 1 茶匙
　　　水 1 湯匙
　　　蔴油 1 茶匙

製法：

* 椰菜花及西蘭花洗淨切成小棵一同浸於鹽水中。
* 羌片切絲。葱，蒜頭切片。
* 凍水煮沸加入鹽，糖，味精及油2湯匙。將兩種菜花放入煨2分鐘，撈起冲凍隔乾水份。
* 鑊燒熱加油 1 湯匙煮沸，洒鹽爆香羌、葱、蒜。倒下椰菜花及西蘭花兜勻炒1分鐘。潛酒 1 茶匙加糖再兜勻上碟。
* 另鑊燒紅，將餘油 1 湯匙煮沸。潛下另 1 茶匙酒，傾入上湯煮沸，再加淡奶及餘下調味料和勻。以生粉水埋饂，拌入蔴油淋在菜花上即可上碟。

Ingredients:

10 oz (280 g) cauliflower
10 oz (280 g) broccoli
4 cups salted water
2 slices ginger
1 shallot
1 garlic clove
4 cups water
1 tbsp salt
1 tbsp sugar
½ tsp M.S.G.
4 tbsp corn oil

Seasoning-
¼ tsp salt
2 tsp wine
1 tsp sugar
½ cup stock
½ cup milk
a pinch of pepper

Gravy Mix-
1 tsp cornflour
1 tbsp water
1 tsp sesame oil

Method:

* *Wash, trim and cut the cauliflower and broccoli into small sprigs then soak in the salted water.*
* *Shred the ginger. Slice the shallot and garlic.*
* *Bring the water to boil with the salt, sugar, M.S.G. and 2 tbsp of the oil. Blanch both vegetables for 2 minutes. Refresh and drain.*
* *Heat the wok with 1 tbsp of the oil then season with the salt and sauté the ginger, shallot and garlic till aromatic. Pour in the vegetables to stir fry for 1 minute. Sizzle half of the wine and add all of the sugar. Toss evenly and dish.*
* *Heat another wok with the remaining oil. Sizzle the rest of the wine and pour in the stock to bring to boil. Add the milk and the rest of the seasoning then thicken the sauce with the gravy mix. Drop in the sesame oil then pour on to the vegetables and dish.*

素 燒 伊 麵

Vegetarian E Fu Noodles

材料：

大伊麵 2 個，
　　每個約 4 安（112克）
沸水 4 杯
白菌 4 安（112克）
菜油 3 湯匙
熟冬菇 2 安（56克）
銀芽 4 安（112克）
蔥頭 1 粒
蒜頭 1 粒

調味—酒 1 茶匙
　　　上湯 ½ 杯
　　　鹽 ¼ 茶匙
　　　生抽 1 茶匙
　　　老抽 ½ 茶匙
　　　糖 1 茶匙
　　　胡椒粉少許
　　　蔴油 1 茶匙

製法：

* 伊麵放於 3 杯沸水中飛水約30秒鐘
  後，撈起轉置水喉下冲洗乾淨，隔
  乾水份。
* 白菌放入餘下 1 杯沸水中飛水，過
  冷河。每隻分切爲 2 份。燒紅鑊加
  油 ½ 湯匙爆香白菌，放置一旁候用
  。
* 熟冬菇切絲。銀芽摘妥。蔥，蒜頭
  拍扁。
* 燒紅鑊加入油 1 湯匙煮沸，爆香蔥
  ，蒜頭棄去。隨即倒入銀芽迅速兜
  炒 8 秒鐘，盛在碟上留用。
* 再將鑊燒紅加入餘油煮沸，傾入伊
  麵及兩種菇類拋匀。潷酒加上湯及
  調味料煮 1 分鐘，拌入銀芽再兜匀
  。試妥味，盛在碟上，即可上桌。

Ingredients:

2 large E Fu noodle cakes, about 4 oz
  (112 g) each
4 cups boiling water
4 oz (112 g) button mushrooms
3 tbsp corn oil
2 oz (56 g) cooked Chinese mushrooms
4 oz (112 g) bean sprouts
1 shallot
1 garlic clove

Seasoning-
1 tsp wine
½ cup stock
¼ tsp salt
1 tsp light soy
½ tsp dark soy
1 tsp sugar
a pinch of pepper
1 tsp sesame oil

Method:

* Blanch the noodles in 3 cups of the
  boiling water for 30 seconds then
  refresh under a running tap and
  drain.
* Blanch the button mushrooms in
  the remaining cup of boiling water
  and refresh. Cut them in halves.
  Heat a wok with ½ tbsp of the oil
  to sauté the button mushrooms
  and leave aside for later use.
* Shred the cooked mushrooms and
  trim the bean sprouts. Mash the
  shallot and garlic.
* Heat the wok and bring 1 tbsp of
  the oil to boil. Sauté the mashed
  shallot and garlic then discard.
  Pour in the bean sprouts to stir fry
  for 8 seconds. Remove on to a
  platter.
* Reheat the wok with the remaining oil. Pour in the noodles
  and the two types of mushrooms
  to toss evenly. Sizzle the wine, add
  the stock and seasoning to simmer
  for a minute. Stir in the bean
  sprouts and season to taste. Dish
  and serve.

八　寶　辣　醬

Vegetarian Eight Treasures

材料：

熟冬菇 6 隻　　　青瓜 3 安（84 克）
紅蘿蔔 2 安（56 克）　青椒 2 安（56 克）
豆腐乾 2 件　　　紅椒 1 安（28 克）
沸水 2 杯　　　葱頭 1 粒
麵筋 4 安（112 克）　蒜頭 1 粒
炸油½鑊　　　菜油 2 湯匙
馬蹄 3 安（84 克）　南乳花生½杯

調味—鹽¼茶匙
　　　辣豆瓣醬 2 湯匙
　　　酒 1 茶匙
　　　水 2 湯匙
　　　甜醬 1 茶匙
　　　老抽 1 茶匙
　　　糖 1 茶匙
　　　胡椒粉少許

饙料—生粉¼茶匙
　　　水 1 茶匙
　　　蔴油 1 茶匙

製法：

＊　熟冬菇切粒，放置一旁候用。
＊　紅蘿蔔及豆腐乾洗淨皆切粒，放入
　　沸水中飛水撈起，過冷河隔乾水份
　　。
＊　麵筋亦切粒，放炸油中炸至金黃色
　　，撈起隔淨餘油。
＊　馬蹄及青瓜去皮切粒。青紅椒去籽
　　皆切粒。葱，蒜頭切片。
＊　燒紅鑊加油煮沸，洒鹽爆香葱，蒜
　　片。傾下青，紅椒及馬蹄炒20秒鐘
　　，即加豆瓣醬及各粒（花生除外）
　　兜勻。濽酒加水及調味料。試妥味
　　後，以生粉水埋饙。將花生倒入拋
　　勻。拌入蔴油上碟即成。

Ingredients:

6 cooked Chinese mushrooms
2 oz (56 g) carrots
2 pieces spiced beancurd
2 cups boiling water
4 oz (112 g) gluten rolls
½ wok hot oil for deep frying
3 oz (84 g) water chestnuts
3 oz (84 g) cucumber
2 oz (56 g) capsicums
1 oz (28 g) chillies
1 shallot
1 garlic clove
2 tbsp corn oil
½ cup toasted peanuts

Seasoning-
¼ tsp salt
2 tbsp hot broadbean paste
1 tsp wine
2 tbsp water
1 tsp sweet paste
1 tsp dark soy
1 tsp sugar
a pinch of pepper

Gravy Mix-
¼ tsp cornflour
1 tsp water
1 tsp sesame oil

Method:

* *Dice the mushrooms and leave aside for later use.*
* *Wash, dice and blanch the carrots and beancurd in the boiling water. Refresh and drain.*
* *Dice the gluten rolls, then deep fry in the boiling oil till golden brown. Remove and drain.*
* *Peel and dice the water chestnuts and cucumber. Deseed and dice the capsicums and chillies. Slice the shallot and garlic.*
* *Bring the oil to boil in a heated wok and sprinkle in the salt. Sauté the shallot and garlic till aromatic. Stir in the capsicums, chillies and water chestnuts to fry for 20 seconds. Add the broadbean paste and all the diced vegetables except the peanuts to mix well. Sizzle the wine, drop in the water and seasoning. Adjust the flavour and thicken the sauce with the gravy mix. Scatter the peanuts to toss evenly. Stir in the sesame oil and serve hot.*

雜 錦 炒 飯

Vegetarian Fried Rice

材料：

青豆¼杯
紅蘿蔔粒¼杯
栗米粒¼杯
沸水 1 杯
鮑魚菇或白菌 2 安（56克）
熟冬菇 1 安（28克）
豆腐乾 1 件
葱頭 1 粒
蒜頭 1 粒
菜油 2 湯匙
蛋白¼杯
凍飯 3 杯

調味—鹽¼茶匙
　　　生抽 1 湯匙
　　　糖¼茶匙
　　　胡椒粉少許

製法：

* 青豆、紅蘿蔔粒及栗米粒放沸水中
　飛水，撈起置水喉下冲凍隔乾水份
　。沸水留起候用。
* 鮑魚菇亦放入以上沸水中飛水，冲
　凍隔乾水份切粒。
* 熟冬菇及豆腐乾皆切粒。葱、蒜頭
　拍扁。
* 燒紅鑊加油 1 湯匙煮沸，洒鹽爆香
　葱、蒜頭棄去。將雜菜粒倒下兜炒
　約30秒鐘，盛起置一旁候用。
* 另鑊以中火燒紅，加入餘油 1 湯匙
　煮沸後轉用慢火倒入蛋白快速炒數
　下，傾下凍飯兜勻。再加其餘配料
　及調料拋勻即可上碟。

Ingredients:

¼ cup sweet peas
¼ cup diced carrots
¼ cup sweet corn kernels
1 cup boiling water
2 oz (56 g) abalone mushrooms or
button mushrooms
1 oz (28 g) cooked Chinese mushrooms
1 piece spiced beancurd
1 shallot
1 garlic clove
2 tbsp corn oil
¼ cup egg white
3 cups cold cooked rice

Seasoning-
¼ tsp salt
1 tbsp light soy
¼ tsp sugar
a pinch of pepper

Method:

* Blanch the sweet peas, carrots and
corn kernels in the boiling water.
Refresh under a running tap and
drain. Keep the boiling water for
later use.
* Blanch the abalone mushrooms in
the same water. Refresh, drain
and dice.
* Dice the cooked mushrooms and
spiced beancurd. Mash the shallot
and garlic.
* Heat the wok with 1 tbsp of oil and
sprinkle the salt. Sauté the garlic
and shallot till aromatic then discard. Pour in the mixed vegetables
to stir fry for 30 seconds. Remove
and leave aside for later use.
* Reheat the wok over medium heat
to bring the remaining oil to boil.
Lower the heat and pour in the egg
white to stir fry briskly. Add the
rice, all the other ingredients and
the seasoning to toss well. Dish
and serve.

素 釀 紮 蹄

Vegetarian Sausage

材料：

腐皮 4 塊	調味—酒 1 茶匙
枝竹 6 安（168克）	上湯 1½ 杯
香鹽 1 茶匙	生抽 1 湯匙
雜菜絲 4 安（112克）	老抽 1 湯匙
菜油 5 湯匙	糖 2 湯匙
沸水 ½ 鑊	味精 ½ 茶匙

烹飪用具—12吋（30公分）丁方扣布
　　　　　2 塊
　　　　　白繩 2 條每條約36吋（90
　　　　　公分）

製法：

* 腐皮抹淨修剪妥當。枝竹洗淨剪成段。
* 雜菜絲加入香鹽拌勻，放置一旁候用。
* 燒紅鑊加入油 2 湯匙，潲酒加上湯及調味料煮沸，將每張腐皮浸入上湯內一拖後取出留用。
* 枝竹放入上湯中以中火煮 3 至 6 分鐘至水份略乾時，取出盛在碟上。
* 腐皮平放桌上，以少許上湯塗勻。疊上第二張腐皮後，即將煮過之枝竹放在一旁，再加雜菜絲捲起。另二張腐皮亦同樣重覆一次。
* 扣布洗淨以餘油塗勻，將腐皮卷放在一邊。以布捲起，另用繩子紮緊。2 條腐皮卷紮妥後，置蒸籠內蒸30分鐘。取出攤凍後除去繩子及扣布切片上碟。

Ingredients:

4 beancurd sheets
6 oz (168 g) beancurd sticks
1 tsp spicy salt
4 oz (112 g) shredded assorted
　vegetables
5 tbsp corn oil
½ wok boiling water

Seasoning-
1 tsp wine
1½ cups stock
1 tbsp light soy
1 tbsp dark soy
2 tbsp sugar
½ tsp M.S.G.

Special Equipment:

2 linen cloths measuring 12 sq. in.
　(30 cm²)
2 strings measuring 36" (90 cm)

Method:

* Clean and trim the beancurd sheets. Wash and section the beancurd sticks.
* Add the spicy salt to the assorted vegetables and mix well. Leave aside for later use.
* Heat the wok with 2 tbsp of oil. Sizzle the wine, pour in the stock and seasoning to bring to the boil. Immerse the beancurd sheet briefly to soften. Remove and put aside.
* Put the beancurd sticks into the boiling stock to simmer over moderate heat for 3 to 6 minutes or until the stock nearly dries up. Dish.
* Lay a piece of beancurd sheet on to the table. Brush with a little of the remaining sauce. Put the second beancurd sheet on top of the first one then place the cooked beancurd sticks and mixed vegetables on one side of the sheet. Roll it up tightly. Repeat the process and finish all the ingredients to make 2 beancurd rolls.
* Wash, dry and brush the linen cloth with the remaining oil. Arrange the beancurd rolls on one side of the linen. Wrap up the beancurd rolls and tie them up tightly with the piece of string. Repeat the process with the other beancurd roll. Cook in a steamer over the boiling water for 30 minutes. Leave to cool. Remove the cloths and strings then slice the beancurd rolls into thin pieces to serve.

素 製 上 湯

Vegetarian Stock

材料：

大豆芽 1 磅（½公斤）
紅蘿蔔½磅（224克）
乾草菰 1 安（28克）
沸水 2 杯
菜油 3 湯匙
冬菇蒂 4 安（112克）
薑 1 片

調味—酒 1 茶匙
　　　水16杯
　　　鹽 4 茶匙

製法：

* 大豆芽摘去根洗淨，以白鑊烙 2 分
  鐘至乾，放置一旁候用。
* 紅蘿蔔去皮切片。
* 乾草菰洗淨放於 1 杯沸水中浸透，
  剪去硬蒂。揸乾水份加油 1 湯匙略
  撈候用。
* 冬菇蒂洗淨修剪妥當，放於餘下 1
  杯沸水中浸至軟。
* 燒紅鑊加入餘油 2 湯匙,煮沸，爆香
  薑片。將豆芽傾下炒透。潷酒加水
  ，紅蘿蔔，草菰及冬菇蒂，蓋上鑊
  蓋慢火煮40分鐘。加調味料試妥味
  後隔去渣留作煮素菜用。

Ingredients:

1 lb (½ kg) soya bean sprouts
½ lb (224 g) carrots
1 oz (28 g) dried straw mushrooms
2 cups boiling water
3 tbsp corn oil
4 oz (112 g) mushroom stalks
1 slice ginger

Seasoning-
1 tsp wine
16 cups water
4 tsp salt

Method:

* *Trim and clean the bean sprouts.
  Parch in a heated dry wok for 2
  minutes. Remove.*
* *Peel and slice the carrots.*
* *Wash and soak the straw mushrooms in 1 cup of the boiling
  water. Trim and squeeze out the
  excess water then marinate with 1
  tbsp of the oil.*
* *Clean, trim and soak the
  mushroom stalks in the remaining
  boiling water until soft.*
* *Heat the wok with the remaining 2
  tbsp of the oil. Sauté the ginger
  until aromatic. Stir in the bean
  sprouts to fry thoroughly. Sizzle
  the wine, add the water, carrots,
  straw mushrooms and the mushroom stalks. Cover to simmer
  over low heat for 40 minutes.
  Season to taste. Remove the
  sediment through a strainer and
  keep the stock for future use.*

雜 菜 米 粉

*Vermicelli with Preserved
Vegetables*

雜 菜 米 粉
Vermicelli with Preserved Vegetables

材料：

米粉 8 安（224克）
沸水 4 杯
梅菜 3 安（84克）
菜油 3 湯匙
青椒 2 安（56克）
紅蘿蔔 2 安（56克）
豆腐乾 2 件

熟冬菇 4 隻
酸羗 2 安（56克）
花生 ¼ 杯
葱頭 1 粒
蒜頭 1 粒
芫茜 2 棵
上湯 3½ 杯

1

2

3

4

調味—鹽 ¼ 茶匙
　　　糖 1 茶匙
　　　上湯 ½ 杯
　　　蠔油 ½ 茶匙
　　　胡椒粉少許

饋料—生粉 1 茶匙
　　　水 1 湯匙
　　　老抽 ½ 茶匙
　　　蔴油 1 茶匙

製法：

* 米粉放沸水中飛水，撈起過冷河隔乾水份。沸水留起候用。
* 梅菜洗淨切粒，用油 ½ 湯匙撈勻。
* 青椒去籽切粒，以另 ½ 湯匙油爆香盛起。紅蘿蔔去皮切粒放於以上沸水中飛水，取出隔去水份留用。
* 豆腐乾，熟冬菇及酸羌全部皆切粒。
* 花生烘脆剁碎。葱蒜頭拍扁。芫茜洗淨摘芡。
* 燒紅鑊加油 1 ½ 湯匙，傾入上湯煮沸。放下米粉煮 1 分鐘，即將米粉及上湯倒入大碗中。
* 另鑊燒熱加入餘油 ½ 湯匙煮沸，洒鹽爆香葱蒜頭棄去。倒入梅菜，糖及其他材料（花生碎例外）迅速兜勻。再加上湯調妥味後，以生粉水埋饋淋在米粉上。洒下花生碎，以芫茜點綴上桌。

Ingredients:

8 oz (224 g) vermicelli
4 cups boiling water
3 oz (84 g) preserved vegetables
3 tbsp corn oil
2 oz (56 g) capsicums
2 oz (56 g) carrots
2 pieces spiced beancurd
4 cooked Chinese mushrooms
2 oz (56 g) pickled ginger
¼ cup peanuts
1 shallot
1 garlic clove
2 parsley sprigs
3½ cups stock

Seasoning-
¼ tsp salt
1 tsp sugar
½ cup stock
1 tsp oyster sauce
a pinch of pepper

Gravy Mix-
1 tsp cornflour
1 tbsp water
½ tsp dark soy
1 tsp sesame oil

Method:

* *Blanch the vermicelli in the boiling water. Refresh and drain. Retain the boiling water for later use.*
* *Clean and dice the preserved vegetables. Mix evenly with ½ tbsp of the oil.*
* *Deseed, dice and sauté the capsicums with another ½ tbsp of oil. Peel, dice and blanch the carrots in the above boiling water. Rinse and drain.*
* *Dice the beancurd, mushrooms and pickled ginger.*
* *Toast and chop the peanuts. Mash the shallot and garlic. Clean and trim the parsley.*
* *Heat the wok with 1½ tbsp of the oil and pour in the stock to bring to the boil. Put in the vermicelli to simmer for 1 minute. Remove the vermicelli and the stock into a big bowl.*
* *Reheat the wok with the remaining ½ tbsp of oil then sprinkle in the salt. Sauté the shallot and garlic then discard. Stir in the preserved vegetables, sugar and the other ingredients except the chopped peanuts to fry briskly. Add the stock and season to taste. Thicken the sauce with the gravy mix then scoop over the vermicelli. Scatter the chopped peanuts on top and garnish with the parsley.*

Beancurd Utensils

豆腐用具

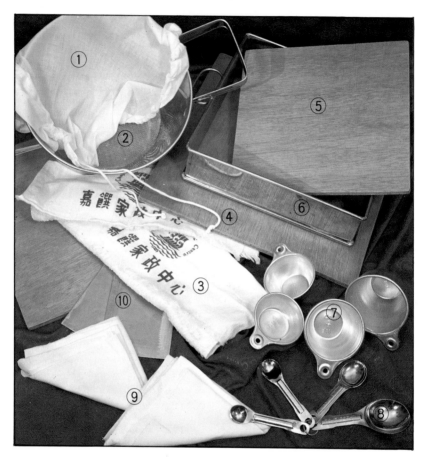

1.	Muslin bag	紗布袋
2.	Stainless steel sieve	鋼篩
3.	2 towels	毛巾
4.	2 pieces 12″ × 12″ planks	12吋丁方木板2件
5.	1 piece 9¾″ × 9¾″ planks	9¾吋丁方木板1件
6.	10 inch square rack	10吋丁方鋼方格
7.	Measuring cups	量杯
8.	Measuring spoons	量匙
9.	2 pieces muslin 20″ × 20″	紗布2塊
10.	2 pieces Beancurd cutter	豆腐刀2塊

Order Form will be sent upon request.

訂貨單請寄本中心郵購部索取

Beancurd Jelly Utensils

豆腐花用具

1.	Stainless steel mixing bowl	鋼桶
2.	Sieve	鋼篩
3.	Muslin bag	紗布
4.	Muslin	紗布
5.	Measuring Cups	量杯
6.	Beancurd Jelly Scoop	豆花壳
7.	Beancurd Jelly Scoop	豆花壳
8.	Measuring Spoons	量匙
9.	2 towels	毛巾

Order Form will be sent upon request.

訂貨單請寄本中心郵購部索取

Our Cooking Centre

Chinese Cookery Courses

Chinese Dishes Course
Chinese Roasts Course
Dim Sum Course
Cakes & Pastries Course
Professional Bread-making Course
Bean Curd Course
Moon Cake Course
Piping Course
Wedding Cake Course
Ingredients Course
Banquet Dishes Course
Vegetable Carving Course
Deep Fried Pastry Course

* * * * * * *

½-3 days Tourist Group Course
1 day Selected Course
1-week Tourist Course
4-week Intensive Course
8-week Intensive Course
13-week Professional Course
17-week Teacher Training Course

Length of course:–
    2 hours to 17 weeks

Our Hostel

* Air-conditioning
* Colour T.V.
* Private bath
* Private telephone
* Reasonable rent

各式烹飪班

各省中菜班
初高燒烤班
初高點心班
高級西餅班
職業麵包班
馳名豆腐班
速成月餅班
速成唧花班
結婚禮餅班
各式原料班
筵席大菜班
蔬菓雕花班
各式油器班
1/2—3天集體遊客班
1天各科精選班
1週遊客班
4週速成班
8週速成班
13週職業班
17週教師訓練班

宿舍設備

＊空氣調節
＊彩色電視
＊私家浴室
＊私人電話
＊合理價錢

Chinese Cookery Terms

1. **To BAKE** is to cook with dry heat, or to dry food with heat.
2. **To BARBEQUE** is to cook meat over a charcoal or wood fire.
3. **To BIND** is to add egg, liquid or melted fat to a mixture in order to hold it together.
4. **To BLANCH** is to immerse the food in boiling water for a short time (from 10 seconds to 5 minutes) in order to tighten the texture, set the colour, or get rid of any unpleasant smell of the food.
5. **To BOIL** is to cook the food in hot bubbling liquid.
6. **To BRAISE** is to finish cooking in a tightly covered wok or saucepan.
7. **To CRIMP** is to slash the surface of a fish at intervals.
8. **To DEEP FRY** is to cook food in a large amount of hot boiling oil in order to make it crispy.
9. **To DOUBLE-BOIL** is to cook in a covered container, which is placed in a covered wok half-filled with boiling water.
10. **To DRAIN** is to remove excess liquid from the ingredients through a strainer or colander.
11. **To DREDGE** is to sprinkle the ingredient with flour or sugar, etc.
12. **To FRY** is to cook with a little hot oil.
13. **To GUT** is to remove the intestine and clean the inside of a fish.
14. **To PARBOIL** is to leave the food in warm oil until half-cooked.
15. **To PARCH** is to brown food in a dry hot wok or frying pan.
16. **To POACH** is to simmer food gently in a liquid which is kept just below boiling point.
17. **To REFRESH** is to rinse the ingredient with cold water after it is blanched. The ingredient is then reheated before serving.
18. **To ROAST** is to prepare the food by using high heat, with flame or over the charcoal.
19. **To SAUTÉ is to stir the ingredients quickly in a wok or pan with a little hot oil, over high heat.**
20. **To SCALD** is to plunge the ingredient into boiling water quickly to make peeling easier or to clean or loosen the hair on the ingredient.
21. **To SHALLOW FRY** is to cook the food in a little oil until both sides are brown.
22. **To SIMMER** is to cook the food or liquid slowly over low heat.
23. **To SMOKE** is to place the food on a rack in a wok or oven filled with smoke.
24. **To STEAM** is to cook the food by putting it into a steamer placed in a wok half-filled with boiling water. Timing begins when the water boils. High heat should be used so that there is enough steam to cook the food quickly.
25. **To STEW** is to cook the food with a little liquid over low heat.
26. **To STIR FRY** is to cook the food quickly in a little oil over medium heat.
27. **To TOSS** is to mix the ingredients evenly by throwing them in a wok and jerking the wok up and down.

The cooking oil used in this book can either be corn oil, vegetable oil, peanut oil or sunflower oil, unless otherwise stated.

烹飪常用術語

焗　—將食物放鑊中蓋密，以文火焗熟。或將拌妥粉料放焗爐中以慢火焗至鬆發。

炭燒　—將食物以叉叉着或放在炭上之鐵網直接以明火燒熟。

搞　—加水或蛋或牛奶在乾材料中和成一糰。

飛水　—將食物放入沸水內稍拖一下，取出洗淨續煮。

烚　—將食物放入沸水中，藉沸水熱力使食物煮熟。與灼及煮略同。灼要手快。

紅燒　—用豉油及水將食物煮熟。與煮及炆略同，有時則與烤之意義相近如燒烤。

炸　—將大量油煮沸，放入食物浸過面，以沸油之熱度使食物炸至酥脆。油炸食品多需上乾粉或濕粉，並要猛油落鑊。

燉　—將食物加配料及水放在燉盅內，再轉放深鍋中加水慢火燉至食品酥爛。食前加調味。此法可保原味，多與補品同燉。

上粉　—將食物以麵粉或糖洒勻在週圍而後按實。

炒　—將鑊燒紅，加少量油煮沸，放入材料迅速兜勻。

泡油　—將食物醃好後，放入猛鑊陰油中泡至油將沸時撈起，隔去油候用。

烙　—以燒熱乾鑊將已洗淨材料文火煮乾後續烙至淺黃色。

浸　—用湯或油煮沸後將火降至將沸未沸之溫度，把食物如鷄或魚等放入，以一定之溫度浸至熟，切不可用猛火。

過冷河　—將食物先用沸水煮過，取出再放冷水中冲洗使其爽脆，麵食多須過冷河。

烤　—以明火將食物炙熟使香氣四溢，用中式烤爐與西式焗爐皆可。

爆　—迅速用猛火將食物以油或醬料加料頭用火逼熟。

灼或燙　—將食物迅速放入沸水中浸片刻然後去皮或拔毛。

煎　—燒紅鑊放少量油將食物僅浸到少許，慢火煎至兩面金黃香脆。

燴　—燒熱油鑊，濟酒加上湯，再加已泡油或煮熟之食物及配料煮沸，以粟粉開水少許打鑷。

烟或燻　—食物先用調味品醃過，排在已放燻料（糖、蔗片、茶葉等）之鑊中的鐵絲網上。蓋上鑊蓋，藉燻料冒出之烟使食物燻至微黃而有烟味。

蒸　—將食物以碟盛起放蒸籠內蓋密，轉置沸水鑊中以蒸氣使食物致熟。

炆　—先將食物放配料爆炒過，轉放另一密蓋鑊內加水少許，改用文火經長時間炆至食物酥爛汁濃爲止。紅炆者熟後加老抽。

拌炒　—此爲中國烹飪中最常用之方法，將食物先泡嫩油至七分熟，然後再燒紅鑊加配料放食物濟酒，迅速勻上碟。

拋　—將鑊中食物迅速在大火上拋動，使火力平均。

煮　—將食物放入水中煮，藉沸水之熱力將食品煮至酥爛，然後加調味料。

保　—將食物放入水中煮滾，改用文火繼續保至夠火及出味爲止。此法通常需時較長。

滷　—用水加滷水料、生抽、紹酒、冰糖等煮至出味。然後把食物飛水後浸在滷水中。浸至入味。滷水盆如處理得宜可長期不變壞。

煨　—將食物放入上湯內慢火煮之，使其吸收上湯味道，或放羗葱水內煨之，以除腥味。

撈拌　—把已煮熟之食物切絲與其他配料放在一起和勻謂之撈。多用於冷盆。

扒　—手法與燴略同，唯汁水較少及較濃。

註：本書食譜內所用之油通常爲粟米油，亦可用菜油或花生油。

"CHOPSTICKS RECIPES"

is a symbol of   CONFIDENCE

Discover the secret of genuine Chinese cooking the CHOPSTICKS way

Chopsticks Recipes Introduction 美味佳肴 綜合食

Chopsticks Recipes Dim Sum 美味佳肴 點心

Chopsticks Recipes Traditional Dishes 美味佳肴 古洋菜

Chopsticks Recipes Quick Meals 美味佳肴 省時快餐

Chopsticks Recipes Everyday Menus 美味佳肴 每日菜

Chopsticks Recipes Cakes and Bread 美味佳肴 西餅麵

Chopsticks Recipes Vegetarian Dishes 美味佳肴 養生膳

More Steps in Chinese Cooking Recipes for Parents and Children 美食入門

First S Chines Recipes for P

CHOPSTICKS PUBLICATIONS
a symbol of confidence

The **Chopsticks Recipes** series English-Chinese bilingual edition (128 pp 105 gsm matt art paper) is an encyclopedia to Chinese cuisine, written for people who enjoy trying different kinds of Chinese food in their daily life. Book 1 is an introduction to a variety of cooking while each of the other 11 books contain one specific subject.

Book 1   —   **introduction**
Book 2   —   **Dim Sum**
Book 3   —   **Traditional Dishes**
Book 4   —   **Quick Meals**
Book 5   —   **Everyday Menus**
Book 6   —   **Cakes and Bread**
Book 7   —   **Vegetarian Dishes**
Book 8   —   **More Dim Sum**
Book 9   —   **Budget Meals**
Book 10 — **Chinese Casseroles**
Book 11 — **Healthy Bean Dishes**
Book 12 — **Vegetable Carvings**

First Steps in Chinese Cooking and **More Steps in Chinese Cooking** English-Chinese bilingual edition (96 pp 115 gsm matt art paper) each contains 42 specially written recipes which have been tested by children from the ages of 8 to 14 years. These book are designed for parents and children to learn Chinese cooking together.

Other Chopsticks publications include **Chopsticks Cookery Cards** Grades 1 and 2 English-Chinese bilingual edition (260 gsm B/S coated art board with pp lamination)

Chopsticks Recipes revised English Edition (128 pp 128 gsm matt art paper)

Chopsticks Wok Miracles English-Chinese bilingual edition (128 pp 128 gsm matt art paper)

Vegetarian Ingredients

素菜材料

1.	Beancurd sheet	腐皮	13.	Cucumber	青瓜
2.	Bean sprouts	芽菜	14.	Carrot	紅蘿蔔
3.	Gluten balls	麵筋	15.	Taro	芋頭
4.	Beancurd balls	豆卜	16.	Green leeks	韮菜花
5.	Soft beancurd	豆腐	17.	Celery	西芹
6.	Spiced pre. vegetable .	冬菜	18.	Towel gourd	絲瓜
7.	Hot broadbean paste	豆瓣醬	19.	Red chillies	紅椒
8.	Winter melon	冬瓜	20.	Walnut	合桃
9.	Preserved mustard ...	榨菜	21.	Bean threads	粉絲
10.	Jicama	沙葛	22.	Chinese mushrooms ...	冬菇
11.	String beans	豆角	23.	Black fungus	木耳
12.	Lotus root	蓮藕	24.	Ginkgo nuts	白菓